ADVENTURING
through the
GENERAL
EPISTLES

A Bible Handbook on the New Testament Letters

ADVENTURING
through the
GENERAL
EPISTLES

RAY C. STEDMAN

DISCOVERY HOUSE
PUBLISHERS®

Adventuring through the General Epistles
© 2009 by Elaine Stedman
All rights reserved.

Discovery House Publishers is affiliated with RBC Ministries, Grand Rapids, Michigan.

Discovery House books are distributed to the trade exclusively by Barbour Publishing, Inc., Uhrichsville, Ohio.

Requests for permission to quote from this book should be directed to: Permissions Department, Discovery House Publishers, P.O. Box 3566, Grand Rapids, MI 49501.

Unless otherwise indicated, Scripture quotations are from the HOLY BIBLE: NEW INTERNATIONAL VERSION®. NIV® Copyright © 1973, 1978, 1984 by International Bible Society. Used by permission of Zondervan.

Interior design by Veldheer Creative Services

ISBN: 978-1-57293-312-5

Printed in the United States of America

09 10 11 12 / DPI / 10 9 8 7 6 5 4 3 2 1

CONTENTS

INTRODUCTION:
LETTERS *to the* CHURCH

THE PURPOSE OF DIVINE REVELATION is nothing less than the transformation of human lives. We should not merely read the Bible. We should experience it, and our contact with it should change our lives. If the Bible isn't changing us, then there is something drastically wrong with the way we are approaching this book.

The Bible is a living book with a living message that God gave us to transform the way we live, and it takes the entire book to do the whole job. The purpose of the Old Testament is to prepare us for truth, and the purpose of the New Testament is to help us realize that truth. In the New Testament, the Gospels and Acts present us with the person and work of Jesus Christ, both in His earthly body and in His body of believers, the church. Following the Gospels and Acts are the Epistles (or letters), which are the explanation of Jesus Christ and the Christian way of living. The letters of Paul, or the Pauline Epistles, are Romans, 1 and 2 Corinthians, Galatians, Ephesians, Philippians, Colossians, 1 and 2 Thessalonians, 1 and 2 Timothy, Titus, and Philemon. Following them we have what are called the General Epistles: Hebrews; James; 1 and 2 Peter; 1, 2, and 3 John; and Jude. The last book of the Bible, Revelation, is the final chapter of biblical revelation. It is not only the story of the end of history and the culmination of God's plan but also contains the only letters written to us by our risen Lord—the seven letters to the first-century churches.

When we come to the Epistles—which occupy the largest part of the New Testament—we are dealing not with preparation or fulfillment but with experience. These letters of the New Testament are the nuts and bolts of the Christian life. They tell us all that is involved in mastering the mystery of Christ and the Christian life. There are depths and heights in Jesus Christ that no mind can grasp—depths to understanding Him and depths to following Him. Through these letters, written by a number of apostles (though most of them were written by the apostle Paul), the Holy Spirit shows us how to discover and explore the deep truths and the deep experience of knowing and following Jesus Christ.

> These letters of the New Testament are the nuts and bolts of the Christian life.

The Epistles are focused around three themes. Romans, 1 and 2 Corinthians, and Galatians deal with the theme "Christ in you." Although that phrase, "Christ in you, the hope of glory," is found in Colossians 1:27, it is really the theme of Romans through Galatians and is the transforming principle of the Christian life. This is what makes Christians different from all other human beings on earth: Christ lives in us. Paul's first four epistles develop this theme.

Ephesians, Philippians, Colossians, 1 and 2 Thessalonians, 1 and 2 Timothy, Titus, and Philemon gather around the theme "you in Christ"— that is, your life in relationship to the rest of the body of Christ. Here you have the church coming into view—the fact that we no longer live our Christian lives as individuals. (For in-depth study of the Pauline Epistles (Romans through Philemon) see the companion volume, *Adventuring Through Paul's Epistles: A Bible Handbook on the New Testament Letters*.)

Hebrews; James; 1 and 2 Peter; 1, 2, and 3 John; and Jude focus on the theme of "how to walk by faith."

This great span of epistles is designed to make all the mighty truths of God available to us in terms of practical experience.

ADVENTURING
through the
GENERAL EPISTLES

CHAPTER ONE

HEBREWS *through* JUDE: ALL *about* FAITH

L ARRY KING, THE FAMOUS CNN talk-show host, once found himself in an unusual position—being the interviewee instead of the interviewer. He was appearing on David Letterman's show, and during their conversation, Letterman asked King, "If you could interview any person from history, who would it be?"

Instantly King replied, "Jesus Christ."

Letterman was so surprised that it took him several seconds to ask a follow-up question: "Well, what would you ask Him?"

"Oh, a lot of questions," King responded, "but my first question would be, 'Were you really born of a virgin?' The answer to that question would define history."

That's true, isn't it? The answer to that question really does define history. If Jesus was truly born of a virgin, if Jesus was truly born of God, the Word made flesh, then we have something tremendous to believe in, to place our faith and trust in. If not, then faith is meaningless, life is meaningless. Truly our faith must be rooted in reality—the reality of the incarnation, life, death, and resurrection of Jesus Christ—or we have nothing to live for.

Faith is not a magical power or potion. It is not a feeling. It is not a set of doctrines or creeds. Faith is trusting in the ultimate reality of the universe. Faith is the key that opens the door to God. Without faith we cannot reach God or receive salvation from Him. So it is vitally important for us to discover what faith truly is. That is the theme of the epistles of Hebrews through Jude. They tell us all about faith—where faith comes from, what it rests on, how to lay hold of it, and how to live it out in our everyday lives.

> **Faith is the key that opens the door to God.**

Time after time during my many years as a pastor, I have heard people make excuses for either failing to receive Jesus as Savior or for failing to appropriate His power to live the Christian life, and the number one excuse is this: "I just can't believe. I just don't have faith." Yet believing is precisely what human beings are designed to do. The proof is found in this well-known passage:

> *Without faith it is impossible to please God, because anyone who comes to him must believe that he exists and that he rewards those who earnestly seek him (Hebrews 11:6).*

In other words, this is the minimum level of faith: If we do not draw near to God, we cannot be saved. If faith is truly impossible for any human being, then that person is beyond the reach of salvation and redemption, but we know that this is not true. Every human being can believe. That is what we were made for. We were made to be dependent creatures, to seek our life from and place our trust in someone or something much bigger and more powerful than we are.

We continually place our trust in the things around us. We accept by faith that the chair we sit in will support us or that the roof over our heads will not cave in on us. Faith is the automatic response of the human spirit. The problem is that we so easily place our faith in things that let us down. We place our faith in people or systems or false gods and philosophies that lead us to grief or even to destruction.

> We were made to be dependent creatures, to seek our life from and place our trust in someone or something much bigger and more powerful than we are.

The great comedy team of Stan Laurel and Oliver Hardy once made a movie called *Big Business*, in which the comedians completely demolished a house for hilarious effect; they put furniture through windows, battered down a door, destroyed the chimney, smashed vases with a baseball bat, and uprooted trees and shrubs. In order to carry out such mayhem on the screen for a reasonable cost, the producers had to locate a house that was already slated for demolition. They found a suitable old house in the Los Angeles area, and the owners were pleased that their house would be used by the famous comedy team to make one of their exceptionally popular movies.

On the appointed day, the film crew and cast arrived, found the house unlocked, set up their cameras, and started rolling. Within a few hours, they managed to make a complete shambles of the house while the camera operator captured every smash, clatter, and crash on film. As they were almost finished filming, the owner of the ruined house arrived—and flew into a rage. The house Laurel and Hardy were supposed to destroy was the house next door!

The entire film crew sincerely believed that they were destroying the right house. But their misplaced faith resulted in a costly mistake. It is not enough to have sincere faith. We must have faith that is rooted in truth.

But how do we know that the Bible is the truth? Many books have been written on apologetics, the body of evidence that verifies biblical truth by means of reason and historical research. The evidence for our faith is there, it is real, and it is compelling. Clearly, the Christian faith is a reasonable faith, because we serve a logical God who says, "Come now, let us reason together" (Isaiah 1:18). However, I believe that very few people who come to faith are really brought there by reason, rational evidence, and argument. I believe most people come to faith and grow in faith through personal experience.

> Some people say that seeing is believing, but I suggest that it is much more accurate to say that believing is seeing.

Some people say that seeing is believing, but I suggest it is much more accurate to say that believing is seeing. When you believe in Jesus Christ and act on your belief, you begin to experience confirmation of the validity and trustworthiness of your beliefs, and your faith grows stronger and deeper as a result. The more of Jesus you experience, the more clearly you see Him. Believing truly is seeing. It is the principle expressed by the father who asked Jesus to heal his epileptic son:

> *Immediately the boy's father exclaimed, "I do believe; help me overcome my unbelief!" (Mark 9:24).*

You begin with the little particle of faith you have, however weak, however small, and you offer it to God. Honestly say to Him, "Lord, I scarcely have any faith at all, but what little there is, I offer to You, and I will act upon it. Help me to know the truth and believe the truth. Reveal Your truth to me."

As we adventure together through these epistles, the books of Hebrews through Jude, we will learn all about faith.

Hebrews: The Roll Call of Faith

The theme of Hebrews is "What is faith?" And the writer to the Hebrews illustrates the meaning of faith through a series of capsule biographies of Old Testament heroes of the faith such as Moses, Joshua, Melchizedek, and Aaron. All of these stories demonstrate that faith is simply an awareness of certain invisible realities that cannot be perceived by the five senses but that are verified through daily experience with God. As we become increasingly aware of these realities, God expects us to grow in our testing of them and our reliance upon Him. If we don't grow in our faith, we shrink from it. Hebrews warns us not to draw back but rather to plunge fully into our faith in Him.

In Hebrews 11, we encounter the roll call of faith, the great record of men and women who lived by faith and accomplished amazing things for

God. These were ordinary people (like you and me) who did extraordinary things by plugging into the power of God by the simple act of faith. They started out with small faith, acted on their tiny mustard seeds of faith, and nurtured that faith into full bloom by putting it to the test. We see how the faith of these Old Testament people was exercised and stretched until they were able to obey God without having any idea what He had planned for their lives:

> *By faith Abraham, when called to go to a place he would later receive as his inheritance, obeyed and went, even though he did not know where he was going (11:8).*

This event in Abraham's life demonstrates the principle stated in the theme verse of Hebrews:

> *Now faith is being sure of what we hope for and certain of what we do not see (11:1).*

Here is the key principle of faith: Faith is not a matter of being sure of all the factual, logical, footnoted, photographed, notarized evidence that our senses can confirm. It is a matter of being certain of what we do not see. How is that possible? What brings us to the conviction of faith? Simply this: As we act on our little bit of belief, as we grow in our experience of God's reality in our lives, His Word sounds a bell in our hearts, and it rings true. Our experience aligns with the truth of God's Word.

> Our experience aligns with the truth of God's Word.

James: The Work of Faith

The epistle of James is an extremely practical book. You can apply its truths to your life continually, in all of your interactions and relationships. James sets forth what faith does in an active, visible way. The key to James is this famous verse:

> *As the body without the spirit is dead, so faith without deeds is dead (James 2:26).*

In other words, faith isn't really faith until you act upon it. Saying, "I believe" while living as if you don't believe is the same as not believing. Many people think that faith is an attitude or an agreement with a certain statement or doctrine. That's not faith at all. Genuine faith changes us. It affects our behavior, and it controls our actions. Faith that is nothing more than a mental attitude is worthless, dead, of no effect. Faith must venture out, take risks, and change our lives.

Faith isn't really faith until you act upon it.

According to James, genuine faith is active, stands up to temptation, shows no prejudice, is kind and responsive to human needs, speaks blessing and love rather than cursing, spreads peace instead of strife, and teaches patience and prayer. These are the deeds of genuine, active faith that we read about in James.

1 and 2 Peter: Strength for the Trial of Faith

Peter was the apostle whose faith failed in the fire of trial, when his Lord was being taken to the cross. Though Peter had brazenly declared before his fellow disciples that he would never deny Jesus, even if all the other disciples failed Him, it was Peter who ultimately denied Him three times, including one denial with a vile curse. As he crept away into the night, having failed his Lord, he heard the words of Jesus as they burned a hole in his heart: "When you have turned back, strengthen your brothers" (Luke 22:32).

In Peter's two letters, we find the apostle doing exactly that: strengthening other Christians for times of trial and persecution. Christians who truly exercise their faith will find their faith tested and tried, and that is the theme of these letters.

Suffering makes faith tremble. Catastrophe provokes our deepest questions. We ask why. In these two letters, Peter answers that question. Our faith in Christ joins us to the life of Christ, including the suffering of Christ. To reach people in a lost and rebellious world will inevitably cause us pain and persecution. When we become a part of Christ, we become instruments for fulfilling His work in the world.

To reach people in a lost and rebellious world will inevitably cause us pain and persecution.

1, 2, and 3 John: Faith Lived Out in Love

The key verse of all three of these letters, 1 John 3:23, shows the link between a life of faith and a life of Christian love:

This is his command: to believe in the name of his Son, Jesus Christ [that's faith], and to love one another as he commanded us [that's the life of the believer].

That is how faith works. It believes, and that belief produces love. To have faith in God means to manifest the life of God, and God is love. How can we say that we truly have faith in God if we do not love one another as God, in Christ, loved us?

The three intertwined themes of 1 John are walking in the light, manifesting love, and reflecting the life of Christ—light, love, and life. In 2 John, the theme again is love, but here the beloved apostle shows us that love is lived out through obedience to God's truth:

This is love: that we walk in obedience to his commands. As you have heard from the beginning, his command is that you walk in love (v. 6).

In 3 John, the apostle addresses a problem in the church—the problem of people who want to be church bosses. John contrasts those who love one another in the body of Christ versus those who love to be first in the church. So faith and love are intertwined—a person of faith is a person who demonstrates faith through love for others.

Jude: Protecting Our Faith

The book of Jude addresses the perils that threaten our faith. Jude outlines a plan to guard our faith against those subtle forces that try to undermine faith, including the desire to have our own way, the lure of immorality, the trap of greed, the dangers of false authority, divisiveness, and worldly influences. Near the close of his book, Jude gives us an admonition that is very timely for us today:

Build yourselves up in your most holy faith [this is the key] and pray in the Holy Spirit [that's the exercise of faith]. Keep yourselves in God's love [again, the exercise of faith] as you wait for the mercy of our Lord Jesus Christ to bring you to eternal life (vv. 20–21).

To protect our faith, we must exercise it. Like the human body, faith must be exercised to keep it from becoming flabby and unhealthy. We exercise our faith by venturing out, by trusting God and daring great things for Him, by stepping out boldly in service and ministry for Him, by discovering and putting to use those hidden resources of spiritual power and spiritual gifts that God has made available to all those who have faith in Him.

Faith is an adventure—a grand, bold, exciting, thrill-a-minute journey. That is what we discover as we adventure through these books, Hebrews through Jude, and learn all about this daring enterprise that we call faith. By living in these books, we learn to trust in things unseen, to love and serve in ever deeper ways, to guard and exercise our faith; in so doing, we add our names to that glorious roll call of those faithful men and women who have placed their trust in God since the beginning of the world.

NOTES

CHAPTER TWO

HEBREWS:
THE ROLL CALL
of FAITH

THE BASEBALL HALL OF FAME is in Cooperstown, New York. Football's Hall of Fame is in Canton, Ohio. The Basketball Hall of Fame is in Springfield, Massachusetts. But do you know about the hall of fame for heroes of the Christian faith? It's found in the book of Hebrews. We will explore the Hebrews Hall of Heroes when we reach chapter 11 of this rich epistle of faith.

The theme of Hebrews is faith. In fact, Hebrews is one of the three New Testament commentaries on a single Old Testament verse, Habakkuk 2:4, which tells us that "the just shall live by his faith" (KJV). This verse opened the eyes of Augustine and inspired him to become a mighty man of faith. This is the Old Testament verse that ignited a fire in the heart of Martin Luther and began the Protestant Reformation some five hundred years ago. It still ignites our hearts today, and we find this idea explored and amplified in the New Testament books of Romans, Ephesians, and Hebrews. Each of these epistles emphasizes a different aspect of that statement, and all three, viewed together, help us to appreciate the rich and multifaceted applications of that statement, "The just shall live by his faith."

> The theme of Hebrews is faith.

The book of Romans talks about "the just" and tells us what it means to be justified, to be accepted as righteous in Jesus Christ. The book of Ephesians emphasizes the words "shall live," and it tells us how to live as justified people—how to walk in the Spirit, how to allow the life of Jesus to live in us. The book of Hebrews takes up the words, "by . . . faith" and shows us how to lay hold of the life by which we are justified.

The Object of Our Faith

We must understand that faith in itself is meaningless and powerless. Many people have faith in things that not only cannot save but can actually bring about their destruction. The power of faith derives not from faith itself but from the one in whom we invest our faith, the object of our faith, Jesus Christ. This is a source of great confusion among many Christians. I often hear people say, "If I only had enough faith, I could do such and such," as though faith were a commodity sold by the pound.

> It is not the quantity of faith that is important; it's what your faith is fastened to.

Jesus has already made it completely clear that the quantity of faith is of no significance. "I tell you the truth," He said, "if you have faith as small as a mustard seed, you can say to this mountain, 'Move from here to there' and it will move. Nothing will be impossible for you" (Matthew 17:20). It is not the quantity of faith that is important; it's what your faith is fastened to. If it is fastened to Jesus Christ, you have all the power you need to carry out God's will in your life. If it is fastened to anything other than Jesus Christ, then your faith is meaningless.

The book of Hebrews is about faith, but even more importantly, it is about the object of our faith, Jesus Christ. As you read it, you will find that Hebrews is the most Christ-centered book in the New Testament. It focuses on the character and redemptive power of Jesus Christ, which is why it is one of the most healing books to read in times of discouragement, defeat, or depression. If we see Him as He is, we cannot help but be strong in faith.

The Mysterious Origin of Hebrews

The King James Version titles this book, The Epistle of Paul the Apostle to the Hebrews. However, Paul likely would not have written this epistle, and the oldest and most reliable manuscripts refer to it as simply, To the Hebrews. We do not know when it was written or to whom. Internal evidence shows it was written to Jewish Christians with the intention of keeping them from slipping back into the rites and legalism of Judaism, but we don't know whether those Christians lived in Palestine, Asia Minor, Greece, or Rome. The list of prospective authors for Hebrews is long, and it includes Paul, Barnabas, Luke, Clement of Rome, Apollos, Silas, Philip, and Priscilla.

While there are some similarities between Hebrews and Paul's epistles— similarities of language and theology—the contrasts are even greater. In Paul's other epistles, the apostle always signs his name, usually at both the beginning and near the end of each letter:

> Paul, called to be an apostle of Christ Jesus by the will of God . . .
> (1 Corinthians 1:1).

> I, Paul, write this greeting in my own hand (1 Corinthians 16:21).

Paul's name appears in all of his other letters, but it appears nowhere in the book of Hebrews. Moreover, the overall style of the Greek language used throughout Hebrews tends to be more polished and learned than the often colloquial and personal tone of Paul's recognized epistles. Throughout his epistles, Paul claims to be an apostle and eyewitness of

Jesus Christ (due to his experience on the road to Damascus), whereas the writer of Hebrews refers to the gospel as having been "confirmed to us by those who heard" Jesus (Hebrews 2:3). Paul, as an eyewitness of Christ, did not need to have the gospel confirmed to him by another person. Also, the author of Hebrews quotes only from the Greek Old Testament (the Septuagint), whereas Paul often quoted from the Hebrew Old Testament.

> Whoever wrote this magnificent book did so under the inspiration of God, and ultimately it is only His authorship that truly matters.

What does all of this mean? Certainly, the book of Hebrews does not have to be written by Paul to be recognized as powerful, authoritative, and inspired by the Spirit of God. We find God's heart expressed on every page. Whoever wrote this magnificent book did so under the inspiration of God, and ultimately it is only His authorship that truly matters.

The Outline of Hebrews

Now, let's take a look at an overview of the entire book of Hebrews so that we can see the flow of the argument of the book at a glance:

Christ, the Object of Our Faith (Hebrews 1:1–4:13)

1.	Christ, before and above all the prophets	1:1–3
2.	Christ, before and above all angels (His deity and humanity)	1:4–2:18
3.	Christ, before and above Moses	3:1–6
4.	The challenge to enter into God's rest	3:7–4:13

The Superior Work of Christ (Hebrews 4:14–10:18)

5.	The priesthood of Christ versus the priesthood of Aaron and the priesthood of Melchizedek	4:14–7:28
6.	The superior covenant of Christ	8:1–13
7.	The superior sanctuary and sacrifice of Christ	9:1–10:18

The Christian's Walk of Faith (Hebrews 10:19–13:25)

8.	Hold fast to the faith you have received	10:19–39
9.	The definition of faith (key verses of Hebrews)	11:1–3

2|8|16

The First Challengers: The Old Testament Prophets

From Hebrews 1:1 to 10:18, Jesus Christ is compared to a number of other leaders, systems, and religious values in which recipients of this letter once trusted. The contrast between Christ and these other people and systems is presented much like an athletic contest or an elimination match where contestants vie for a championship. Again and again, a challenger rises to confront the hero, Jesus Christ, and one after another, the challenger is vanquished. Again and again, the hero emerges triumphant, superior to all comers. Throughout this letter, Christ, the object of our faith, is compared with all the lesser things in which people place their faith, and every challenger is found wanting. Christ alone is supreme.

> In the past God spoke to our forefathers through the prophets at many times and in various ways, but in these last days he has spoken to us by his Son, whom he appointed heir of all things, and through whom he made the universe (1:1–2).

The writer of Hebrews recalls the prophets who meant so much to the Hebrew mind and heart, the great names of Hebrew history such as Isaiah, Jeremiah, Ezekiel, Daniel, Hosea, and Habakkuk. These prophets lived at the same time as great secular philosophers such as Socrates, Plato, and Aristotle, yet their views of truth and reality far outstripped the thinking of their secular contemporaries. God spoke to them and through them in the past, "but in these last days he has spoken to us by his Son."

Immediately, the writer of Hebrews dismisses the prophets as having no equality with Jesus Christ. After all, they were merely spokesmen and instruments, but Jesus is God himself, enthroned as king of the universe. His life defines the boundaries of history, and He upholds everything by the word of His power. How can a mere prophet compare with Him?

The Second Challengers: The Angels

The next challengers are the angels. In the Greek world of the New Testament church, angels were regarded as important beings. The Greek gods and goddesses were virtually the equivalent of angels in the eyes of the Greeks, powerful supernatural beings who were flawed and limited. The Greek pantheon of deities did not contain a single all-powerful, all-knowing, all-loving supreme being—only a bunch of sub-deities much like the angels of Judeo-Christian theology.

In this passage, the writer to the Hebrews considers the question of who is greater, the angels or the Son of God. He points out immediately that the Son, the Lord Jesus, is superior to any angel:

> *To which of the angels did God ever say,*
> *"You are my Son; today I have become your Father"?*
> *Or again,*
> *"I will be his Father, and he will be my Son"?*
> *And again, when God brings his firstborn into the world, he says,*
> *"Let all God's angels worship him."*
> *In speaking of the angels he says,*
> *"He makes his angels winds, his servants flames of fire."*
> *But about the Son he says,*
> *"Your throne, O God, will last for ever and ever, and righteousness*
> *will be the scepter of your kingdom" (1:5–8).*

God never said to any angel, "You are my Son; today I have become your Father." The Son is superior to the angels, and, what's more, the angels worshiped and obeyed Him. The angels themselves confess that Jesus is superior.

> The angels themselves confess that Jesus is superior.

The Second Adam

In chapters 2 and 3, the writer of Hebrews presents Jesus as the true man, the second Adam. Jesus came to fulfill the destiny of human beings, a destiny lost when Adam threw it away through the first sin. God created human beings to be creatures of splendor and authority; how heartbreaking to think of how much of God's image was lost in the fall! We were originally made to be rulers, king and queens in the universe, a fact that is reflected in Psalm 8:

> *When I consider your heavens, the work of your fingers, the moon and the stars, which you have set in place, what is man that you are mindful of him, the son of man that you care for him? You made him a little lower than the heavenly beings and crowned him with glory and honor.*
> *You made him ruler over the works of your hands; you put everything under his feet (vv. 3–6).*

> God created human beings to be creatures of splendor and authority.

That is God's design for humanity, but our fallen state keeps us from fulfilling it. But Jesus—"the son of man"—is here in this passage, fulfilling our original destiny, living out our unfallen potential, sitting at the right hand of God. He is the true man—humanity as God intended us to be. We are higher than the angels because God created us to be higher than the angels. God said of humanity, "Let us make man in our image." He did not say that about any angel—only of men and women, you and me. So Jesus—the Son of Man, the perfect human being, the Second Adam—is superior to the angels.

The book of Hebrews contains five warnings, and at this point we encounter the first one:

The First Warning

> *We must pay more careful attention, therefore, to what we have heard, so that we do not drift away. For if the message spoken by angels was binding, and every violation and disobedience received its just punishment, how shall we escape if we ignore such a great salvation? This salvation, which was first announced by the Lord, was confirmed to us by those who heard him (2:1–3).*

If Jesus is greater than the prophets and the angels, says Hebrews, then we ought to listen to Him. If prophets have affected the stream of history as much as they have and the angels are the invisible agents of God working through all of history, then surely we ought to listen to the Son. Do not neglect to listen!

The Next Challengers: Moses and Joshua

The next challengers who move into the picture are Moses and Joshua, great people of God whom God greatly used. The Hebrew people almost idolized them as supreme examples of people mightily used of God. In chapter 3, Jesus is compared to Moses; in chapter 4, He is compared to Joshua. What is the writer's argument? Simply this: Moses was a servant in the house of God. Jesus, however, is the Son to whom the house belongs and for whom it is built. Obviously, He has the supremacy.

As a boy in Montana, I was invited to visit a ranch owned by a wealthy family. The invitation came not from the family but from one of the hired hands. He drove me to the ranch, and as we drove toward the imposing two-story ranch house, he turned toward the bunkhouse out back.

"What's it like in that big house?" I asked.

"I dunno," the ranch hand said. "Never been in there. That house belongs to the owner and his family. I can't take you in there."

Sometime later, I saw a beautiful palomino horse in the pasture, and I said, "Gee, I'd sure love to take a ride on that horse."

"Sorry, boy," said the ranch hand. "You can't ride that horse. It belongs to the family." All day long I was frustrated because everything I wanted to do he couldn't let me do because he was only a hired worker.

Later, I got to know the son of that family, a boy my own age, and everything changed. We rode that palomino horse all over, and we went into the house and had the complete run of the place. We even went into the kitchen and helped ourselves to the refrigerator! We made ourselves at home. Why? Because a son has greater liberty than a servant.

Moses was just a servant, but Jesus was the master. Moses led the people of God out of Egypt toward the land of Canaan, which symbolized the place of God's rest, the rest and peace God wants all of us to experience through faith in Jesus Christ. Moses led his people toward a symbol of the rest of God, but Jesus leads all people into the actual place of rest.

That rest is defined for us in Hebrews 4:9–10:

> *There remains, then, a Sabbath-rest for the people of God; for anyone who enters God's rest also rests from his own work, just as God did from his.*

The point is this: If you stop depending upon yourself and your own effort, you have learned to enter into rest because you start depending on God's work in you. That is the lost secret of humanity. That is the secret that Adam and Eve lost in the Garden of Eden and the one Jesus Christ came to restore to us. When we learn to live by the work of God in us instead of by our own work, we experience lives that are peaceful, calm, trusting, powerful, and undisturbed by circumstances, so we can accomplish great things for Christ's sake. The paradox of this principle is that nothing is more active, effective, and powerful than a life that is lived in God's rest.

> *If you stop depending upon yourself and your own effort, you have learned to enter into rest because you start depending on God's work in you.*

Joshua tried, but he could not lead the people into real rest. He merely took them into the symbol of rest, the land. Only Jesus can give us real rest. Hebrews tells us, "Let us, therefore, make every effort to enter that rest" (4:11), so that we avoid the downfall of those in the wilderness who, through disobedience, fell away and lost out on God's will and blessing for their lives.

The second warning is in Hebrews 3:12–15:

The Second Warning

> See to it, brothers, that none of you has a sinful, unbelieving heart that turns away from the living God. But encourage one another daily, as long as it is called Today, so that none of you may be hardened by sin's deceitfulness. We have come to share in Christ if we hold firmly till the end the confidence we had at first. As has just been said:
>
> "Today, if you hear his voice, do not harden your hearts as you did in the rebellion."

Remember and heed this warning: Do not harden your heart and resist God's leading. Do not say to yourself, "I'm alright the way I am. I'm doing okay. I don't need to make any progress in my relationship with God. I don't need to listen to Him anymore. I don't need to enter into His rest." No, do not harden your heart. Do not resist what God is saying. Let God lead you into His rest.

The Next Challengers: Aaron and Melchizedek   3|1|16

The next challenger to the superiority of Christ is Aaron, the high priest of Israel, along with the whole system of the priesthood. A great deal of this letter has to do with the subject of priesthood. This is significant, because priests have great value. In the Old Testament, the priests had two very important functions: to relieve guilt and to relieve confusion. In Hebrews 5:1–2 we read:

Every high priest is selected from among men and is appointed to represent them in matters related to God, to offer gifts and sacrifices for sins. [That is relief of guilt—to lift the load and burden of sin.] He is able to deal gently with those who are ignorant and are going astray, since he himself is subject to weakness. [That is the relief of confusion—to deal gently with the ignorant and wayward.]

The writer of Hebrews symbolizes Jesus Christ's higher priesthood through a man named Melchizedek. Melchizedek appears in the Old Testament in a very mysterious way. He steps out of the shadows for a moment and deals with Abraham, then returns to obscurity and is never heard from again. The Old Testament refers to Melchizedek several times, but he is a figure of mystery until you read the New Testament. Here in Hebrews, we see what this strange man signified. Melchizedek's characteristics were those of the priesthood Christ has today.

He was instantly available. The story, recorded in Genesis 14, tells of Abraham meeting the king of Sodom after Abraham's defeat of the five kings. Although he did not know it, Abraham was in trouble. The king of Sodom planned to make him a subtle offer that would derail Abraham in his walk of faith. He could not possibly have detected the subtlety of this offer, but then Melchizedek suddenly appeared. He was instantly available.

He was a king without father or mother. This is as far as the record goes in the Old Testament. Here is an Old Testament picture of Christ in His eternal relationship to God.

> The priesthood of Christ is far superior to any other priesthood because Jesus is instantly available, He is eternal, and He provides us with His own infinite power and strength.

He provided the strength of Christ to Abraham, symbolized by the elements of Holy Communion. Melchizedek strengthened Abraham; likewise, Jesus Christ strengthens us. Melchizedek strengthened Abraham by the offering of bread and wine, which in the communion service are the symbols of the body and the blood, the life of the Lord Jesus.

Here in Hebrews, the image of Melchizedek is summoned to represent the priestly ministry of Jesus Christ. The priesthood of Christ is far superior to any other priesthood because Jesus is instantly available, He is eternal, and He provides us with His own infinite power and strength.

In this connection we find a third warning—the warning against delay. This is one of the most serious warnings in the book: — The Third Warning

> Let us leave the elementary teachings about Christ and go on to maturity, not laying again the foundation of repentance from acts that lead to death, and of faith in God, instruction about baptisms, the laying on of hands, the resurrection of the dead, and eternal judgment. And God permitting, we will do so.
>
> It is impossible for those who have once been enlightened, who have tasted the heavenly gift, who have shared in the Holy Spirit, who have tasted the goodness of the word of God and the powers of the coming age, if they fall away, to be brought back to repentance, because to their loss they are crucifying the Son of God all over again and subjecting him to public disgrace (6:1–6).

Although we may have tasted the outward experiences of Christianity and seem to have much that is real in our Christian lives, we must press on into this place of rest and trust in Jesus Christ, or these external evidences of Christianity are of no value to us. Here is a sobering warning: If you trust too long in the untrue, the unreal, the unreliable, a day of desperation will come when you will look for the true, and you will not be able to find it.

The Tabernacle and the Law   3|8

The tabernacle and the law are two more things that people trust in—buildings and self-effort (represented by the law). The writer of Hebrews draws a sharp contrast between the tabernacle and the law on the one hand and Christ on the other. He looks at the old tabernacle in the wilderness and says, "That's just a building symbolizing the real house of God, which is a human life—a man, woman, boy, or girl. God doesn't want to live in buildings; He wants to live in us!"

I like the story of the little boy who was chewing gum in a church building, and a woman said to the pastor, "Look at that boy chewing gum in church. Do you let children chew gum in the house of God?"

"My dear lady," the pastor replied, "it's the house of God that's chewing the gum!" And he is exactly right.

So the old tabernacle or the temple in Jerusalem or a cathedral or a church is nothing but a building. The true house of God is you. We are His house. He dwells in us: "Christ in you, the hope of glory" (Colossians 1:27).

Intimately linked with the Old Testament tabernacle is the Old Testament law: the Ten Commandments and the other laws, rites, and restrictions of the Law of Moses. The Ten Commandments are wonderful, flawless guidelines for human conduct. They fail in practice not because they are flawed but because we are flawed. We are weak and powerless to keep the law's demands. Even when we try our best, all we can achieve is an outward external obedience to avoid punishment, but the heart within is still wrong, and we know it.

The Lord Jesus has a solution to this: *He writes the law on your heart.* He puts the Spirit of God within you to prompt you to love, for love is the fulfillment of the law.

The Fourth Warning

Here we encounter yet another warning: Do not deceive yourself. Do not allow sin to establish a deceitful foothold in your life. If you presume on God's grace this way, the writer of Hebrews says, there will be nothing left for you but a certain end of evil:

> *If we deliberately keep on sinning after we have received the knowledge of the truth, no sacrifice for sins is left, but only a fearful expectation of judgment and of raging fire that will consume the enemies of God. Anyone who rejected the law of Moses died without mercy on the testimony of two or three witnesses. How much more severely do you think a man deserves to be punished who has trampled the Son of God under foot, who has treated as an unholy thing the blood of the covenant that sanctified him, and who has insulted the Spirit of grace? (10:26–29).*

Think of it! At infinite cost—the cost of His own Son—God has provided a way to be righteous before Him, a way to be strengthened within, a way to be preserved strong and pure in the midst of all the decadent influences and adverse circumstances around us. How could we even think of setting all this aside and saying, "No, God, I'm going to make it on my own"? Could anything be more insulting to God? So the writer of Hebrews warns us not to presume on God's grace.

The Hall of Heroes

In the final section of the letter, the writer of Hebrews states the means by which we obtain all that God makes available to us. That means is called faith. In chapter 11, we can learn what faith is, how it behaves, and how to recognize it. The key verse of the entire book of Hebrews is found right here:

> *Now faith is being sure of what we hope for and certain of what we do not see (11:1).*

People are always looking for evidence for the Christian faith. And it is available because Christianity is a reasonable faith, based on the historical fact of the life of Christ and the reality of His resurrection.

But the real evidence for faith comes not from an archaeological dig in Palestine or from the Hubble space telescope or from the pen of a great theologian. It comes from experience. Faith is not a matter of being sure of all the evidence we can see. Faith is a matter of being certain of what we do not see! How do we become certain of something we do not see? By experiencing the reality of God's love and friendship in our daily lives. Seeing is not believing. Believing is seeing. When we make a decision to live by faith—even if we think our faith is weak or nearly nonexistent—God meets us, shows himself to us, and increases our faith through a daily relationship with Him.

In the rest of chapter 11, the writer of Hebrews presents the roll call of faith. And as you read through the wonderful chapter that lists the heroes of faith, you find that faith anticipates the future, acts in the present, evaluates the past, dares to move out, and persists to the end. As you read through this roll call of God's Old Testament faithful, you read the stories of:

- Abel, who by faith made a better sacrifice than his brother, Cain;
- Enoch, who did not taste death because of his faithful service to God;
- Noah, who saved his family from the flood of God's judgment because of his faith in God's word;
- Abraham and Sarah, who followed God by faith, not knowing where God would lead them;

- Isaac, who blessed his sons by faith;
- Jacob, who blessed Joseph's sons by faith;
- Joseph, who foresaw by faith the exodus of Israel from Egypt to the Land of Promise;
- the parents of Moses, who by faith hid their child, the future leader of Israel, from the wrath of Pharaoh;
- Moses, who chose by faith to identify with the suffering of his people, even though he could have chosen the pleasures, wealth, and security of sinful Egypt;
- Joshua, who by faith called down the walls of Jericho;
- Rahab, the prostitute, who received Israel's spies because of her faith in Israel's God;
- and others—Gideon, Barak, Samson, Jephthah, David, Samuel, the prophets, and many other saints unnamed but remembered forever by God for battling by faith to the end of their lives, enduring incredible persecution while trusting in God to provide for them a better resurrection.

It is an incredible record of faith, an inspiring list of heroic accomplishments—ordinary people of faith doing extraordinary things by faith. It is a list of people who, by faith, allowed God to live out His life through theirs.

The Walk of Faith

The final two chapters tell us how faith is produced in our lives and how God makes us strong in the faith so that we can walk the daily Christian walk. First, we are made strong by looking to Jesus:

> *Let us fix our eyes on Jesus, the author and perfecter of our faith,*
> *who for the joy set before him endured the cross, scorning its shame,*
> *and sat down at the right hand of the throne of God (12:2).*

When you look to Jesus, you will not be merely inspired, you will be empowered!

When you read the stories of Abraham, David, Moses, Barak, Samson, Martin Luther, John Wesley, D. L. Moody, Jim Elliot, and C. S. Lewis, you will be inspired. But when you look to Jesus, you will be not merely inspired, you will be empowered! That is why we are told to fix our gaze steadily upon Jesus, the author and the finisher of faith, because He alone can make us strong in our time of weakness.

The writer of Hebrews goes on to say:

> *In your struggle against sin, you have not yet resisted to the point of shedding your blood. And you have forgotten that word of encouragement that addresses you as sons:*
> *"My son, do not make light of the Lord's discipline, and do not lose heart when he rebukes you, because the Lord disciplines those he loves, and he punishes everyone he accepts as a son."*
> *Endure hardship as discipline; God is treating you as sons. For what son is not disciplined by his father? (12:4–7).*

Faith grows through times of trouble, the disciplining season of our lives. God does not enjoy our pain, but He does use pain as a disciplining hand to teach us to exercise our faith. If you never had any problems, how could you exercise faith? If you never experienced lean times and losses, how could you ever learn to depend solely on God? That is why you can be sure you'll have trouble in this life.

But that's not the only way we exercise our faith. We also exercise our faith by encouraging one another in the shining hope that awaits us:

> *You have not come to a mountain that can be touched and that is burning with fire; to darkness, gloom and storm; to a trumpet blast or to such a voice speaking words that those who heard it begged that no further word be spoken to them, because they could not bear what was commanded: "If even an animal touches the mountain, it must be stoned." The sight was so terrifying that Moses said, "I am trembling with fear."*
> *But you have come to Mount Zion, to the heavenly Jerusalem, the city of the living God. You have come to thousands upon thousands of angels in joyful assembly, to the church of the firstborn, whose names are written in heaven. You have come to God, the judge of all men, to the spirits of righteous men made perfect, to Jesus the mediator of a new covenant, and to the sprinkled blood that speaks a better word than the blood of Abel (12:18–24).*

The first paragraph in this passage speaks of the harshness of the law. The law is so strict and so terrifying that no one can bear the weight of it. Even Moses is terrified of it. But we have not been brought to Mount Sinai, a mount of law and fire, smoke and judgment, storm and fear. We have been brought to Mount Zion, a shining city of light, a place of grace and joy where people have been made perfect and where Jesus reigns as the mediator of the new covenant. Isn't that a beautiful word picture of our future with Him? Doesn't that encourage your faith? It does mine.

The Fifth Warning

But linked to this powerful word picture of encouragement is a warning:

See to it that you do not refuse him who speaks. If they did not escape when they refused him who warned them on earth, how much less will we, if we turn away from him who warns us from heaven? At that time his voice shook the earth, but now he has promised, "Once more I will shake not only the earth but also the heavens." The words "once more" indicate the removing of what can be shaken—that is, created things—so that what cannot be shaken may remain (12:25–27).

I believe we are in those times when everything that can be shaken is being shaken. What does this world depend upon? Governments, politics, education, legislation? All of these things are the fundamentals of history, the institutions people invest their hopes in, yet every one of these human institutions is something that can be and will be shaken. Even now, we are facing the times when God is going to allow everything to be shaken that can be shaken. In this entire, vast universe of ours, only one thing exists that cannot be shaken:

Since we are receiving a kingdom that cannot be shaken, let us be thankful, and so worship God acceptably with reverence and awe, for our "God is a consuming fire" (12:28–29).

> The kingdom of God, His rule over our hearts, and the lordship of Jesus Christ in our lives can never be shaken.

The kingdom of God, His rule over our hearts, and the lordship of Jesus Christ in our lives can never be shaken. What are being shaken and tested today are phoniness and deception. What cannot be shaken are truth and faith. These days we see many people who claim to be Christians, who outwardly seem strong in the faith, turning away, falling away, renouncing or betraying their faith when they are shaken or exposed. But the things that cannot be shaken will remain, even while all else crumbles and falls.

A few verses toward the end of Hebrews sum up the meaning of this letter for our lives in these perilous times, in the early years of a new millennium:

> *May the God of peace, who through the blood of the eternal covenant brought back from the dead our Lord Jesus, that great Shepherd of the sheep, equip you with everything good for doing his will, and may he work in us what is pleasing to him, through Jesus Christ, to whom be glory for ever and ever. Amen (13:20–21).*

These words are both a prayer and a blessing. May we carry the peace of our great Shepherd with us no matter where we go, no matter what we face, as we walk the walk of faith.

NOTES

NOTES

Notes

NOTES

CHAPTER THREE

JAMES:
FAITH *in* ACTION

T HE EPISTLE OF JAMES HAS PRESENTED a number of problems to Bible scholars over the years. For example, Martin Luther had trouble accepting James as inspired Scripture, calling it "an epistle of straw." His problem, and the problem of many theologians over the years, has been James's emphasis on works as well as faith. Three times in this letter, James makes a statement such as this one:

> As the body without the spirit is dead, so faith without deeds is dead (2:26).

Some see these words of James as clashing with the emphasis on grace in Paul's epistles, typified by this statement:

> It is by grace you have been saved, through faith—and this not from yourselves, it is the gift of God—not by works, so that no one can boast (Ephesians 2:8–9).

Some look at Paul on the one hand and James on the other and say, "Who should we believe? Is salvation by grace through faith alone, or is faith truly dead without works?" In fact, this is a false dichotomy. Paul and James are both correct. The epistles of Paul and the epistle of James do not contradict each other—they complement each other. Paul is saying that good works cannot save us. Rather, only the grace of God, appropriated by our faith, can save us. James would never argue against Paul's assertion that God's grace alone saves; he presupposes that the reader understands these doctrines that are so clearly stated in Paul's letters.

But James goes a step further. He wants us to also understand a principle that is fully accepted and understood in Paul's letters: Faith means more than simply agreeing with a set of doctrines. Genuine faith involves commitment that is expressed through actions. If we do not demonstrate behavior that is consistent with what we say we believe, then what good is our supposed faith? Faith that is not demonstrated by action is dead indeed! Works cannot save us, but works demonstrate that we do have a saving faith.

Genuine faith involves commitment that is expressed through action.

The book of James—far from being an "epistle of straw"—is the practical application of all the doctrines that Paul sets forth on faith. James is where the rubber meets the road. James is where our faith is expressed in tangible ways through our actions. This epistle is indispensable to our understanding of what our faith is all about and how the Christian life is supposed to be lived. Properly understood, this is one of the most powerful, inspired, life-changing books of the Bible. It is the road map for the walk of faith.

James: Witness to the Deity of His Half Brother, Jesus

James is a book of unique significance to us because it comes from the one who probably knew more about the Lord Jesus than any other human being: James, the half brother of our Lord. The apostle James was raised with Jesus in the same home in Nazareth by Joseph and Mary. He grew up with the Lord Jesus, saw Him through all those silent years of which we have no record, and joined with His three other brothers—Joseph, Simon, and Judas—in opposition to the Lord Jesus during the early days of His ministry. James was converted to faith in Christ, his half brother, by the unmistakable evidence of the resurrection. The apostle Paul tells us that after the resurrection, the Lord appeared to James (1 Corinthians 15:7). What greater evidence could James have asked for than to see the risen Lord in person?

> James was converted to faith in Christ, his half brother, by the unmistakable evidence of the resurrection.

Some people question whether James the brother of Jesus was the James who wrote this letter. But if you look carefully into the background of this letter, you'll find sufficient evidence. In the early days after the resurrection, James, the Lord's brother, became the acknowledged leader of the church in Jerusalem, and he was regarded by all, even the Jews, with reverence and respect, so that he gained the title "James the Just One."

Tradition tells us (as does Eusebius, an early church father and respected historian) that James was finally martyred for his faith by being pushed off the pinnacle of the temple of Jerusalem, the same place where the devil tempted Jesus to jump off. The pinnacle was the point in the wall around the temple that jutted out over the Kidron Valley. From the top of that wall down into the valley is a drop of about a hundred feet. Eusebius tells us that about the year A.D. 66, Jews who had become angered with James the Just for his Christian testimony pushed him off the pinnacle. According to Eusebius, the fall did not kill James, and he managed to stumble to his knees to pray for his murderers. So they finished the job by stoning him to death, and he joined the roll call of martyrs, a hero of the faith.

If you lay this letter of James alongside Jesus' Sermon on the Mount, you'll see more than a dozen exact parallels. So it is evident that James, the writer of this letter, listened to the Lord Jesus and heard these messages, even though he may have struggled with them at the time. This letter, like the teaching of the Lord himself, uses many figures of speech taken from nature—word pictures involving the waves of the sea, the animal kingdom, the forests, the fish, and more—just as Jesus himself did so frequently.

> This letter of James and Jesus' Sermon on the Mount share more than a dozen exact parallels.

James begins his letter with a tremendous testimony to the deity of Christ:

James, a servant of God and of the Lord Jesus Christ,
To the twelve tribes scattered among the nations:
Greetings (1:1).

It is amazing that a man who grew up with Jesus Christ, who had known Him all his life and had once opposed Him, would now address Jesus in this way: "the Lord Jesus Christ." James wrote with a reverence and a respect for the person of the Lord that is unequaled in the New Testament. It is a tremendously powerful and practical message from someone who not only had seen and heard the Lord Jesus but had known Him intimately.

The Outline of James

Here is a structural overview of the epistle of James:

The Testing of Faith (James 1:1–18)

1.	The purpose of testing	1:1–12
2.	The source of temptation	1:13–18

The Operation of Genuine Faith (James 1:19–5:6)

3.	Genuine faith is obedient	1:19–27
4.	Genuine faith is not prejudiced	2:1–13
5.	Genuine faith is demonstrated by good works	2:14–26
6.	Genuine faith controls the tongue	3:1–12
7.	Genuine faith demonstrates wisdom	3:13–18
8.	Genuine faith demonstrates humility	4:1–12
9.	Genuine faith demonstrates reliance on God	4:13–5:6

Faith Hopes, Cares, and Triumphs (James 5:7–20)

How Faith Grows

The theme of this letter is faith. "Without faith," the book of Hebrews tells us, "it is impossible to please God" (Hebrews 11:6). Faith, therefore, is the channel by which all God's blessings come to us, and without faith, all you can do is sin. "Everything that does not come from faith," says the apostle Paul, "is sin" (Romans 14:23). If your actions are not consistent with your Christian faith, then what you are doing is distasteful and disgusting to God, even though people may applaud you.

In this letter, then, the apostle James tells us several things about faith. James 1 answers the question, "What makes faith grow?" Jesus said that it takes very little to constitute faith. If you have faith like a grain of mustard seed—just the tiniest particle of faith—you have enough faith to act upon. Even if your tiny particle of faith is hemmed in with doubts, when you are committed enough to act on that tiny particle of faith, it is enough. Your faith will move mountains.

Two forces in life make faith grow. The first is trials. "Oh, no!" you may be thinking. "Not that!" But it's true. Trials are the fertilizer that makes faith grow. So James 1 is a wonderful chapter for those who are facing trials. James writes,

Trials

> *Consider it pure joy, my brothers, whenever you face trials of many kinds, because you know that the testing of your faith develops perseverance. Perseverance must finish its work so that you may be mature and complete, not lacking anything (1:2–4).*

You need trials. This is a biblical truth. James goes on to describe how to take trials: Accept them, he says, as from God. And that's very hard. It takes a lot of wisdom to be able to accept the trials of life and to know that God wants to use those trials to produce good in our lives. Where does that wisdom come from? James replies:

If any of you lacks wisdom, he should ask God, who gives generously to all without finding fault, and it will be given to him (1:5).

And what is the result of enduring trials while seeking comfort and wisdom from God to withstand those trials? Blessing!

Blessed is the man who perseveres under trial, because when he has stood the test, he will receive the crown of life that God has promised to those who love him (1:12).

What kinds of trials was James talking about here? Stonings, beatings, imprisonment, death, derision, the destruction of entire families—and for what? For something we take for granted in our own society: saying, "Jesus is Lord." Just think of the kinds of "trials" that can absolutely ruin a day today: crabgrass in the lawn or getting cut off in traffic.

Trials teach us lessons we could never learn otherwise. Without the buffeting of trials in our lives, we would be weak, spindly, incomplete Christians, unable to take on the great responsibilities that will be placed upon us in the day we enter into the Lord's kingdom and into the fullness of His service. We see this principle in nature. Butterflies must struggle to break out of their cocoons, and chicks must struggle to break free of their eggs. If we break open the cocoon or the eggshell, thinking we are doing that creature a favor, the butterfly or the baby chick will be weak, sickly, and incomplete for having been spared the struggle of fully emerging through its time of trial. So it is with us and the first instrument God uses to help us grow: trial.

> Without the buffeting of trials in our lives, we would be weak, spindly, incomplete Christians.

God's Word

The second instrument God uses to produce growth is His Word:

Do not merely listen to the word, and so deceive yourselves. Do what it says. Anyone who listens to the word but does not do what it says is like a man who looks at his face in a mirror and, after looking at himself, goes away and immediately forgets what he looks like. But the man who looks intently into the perfect law that gives freedom, and continues to do this, not forgetting what he has heard, but doing it—he will be blessed in what he does (1:22–25).

James reminds us that it is the Word of God that makes our faith grow, particularly as the Word is expressed in our actions. Faith comes by hearing, says the apostle Paul, and hearing by the word of God (see Romans 10:17). The only way to know the great thoughts of God, the deep things of God, the underlying secrets of life, is to spend time with the book that reveals them. So let your faith grow by rejoicing in trial and by understanding and acting on God's Word.

Making Faith Visible

In chapters 2 and 3, James shows us how to take something as intangible and invisible as faith and make it solid and visible. He gets down to practical realities and suggests three visible indications that a person's faith is real.

First, there must be no partiality or prejudice. If a person is prejudiced against others because of their race or the state of their bank accounts, he or she has no real faith. If a person treats others as unimportant because of their low social status or lack of influence, then that person has no real faith. James writes,

No Prejudice

> My brothers, as believers in our glorious Lord Jesus Christ, don't show favoritism. Suppose a man comes into your meeting wearing a gold ring and fine clothes, and a poor man in shabby clothes also comes in. If you show special attention to the man wearing fine clothes and say, "Here's a good seat for you," but say to the poor man, "You stand there" or "Sit on the floor by my feet," have you not discriminated among yourselves and become judges with evil thoughts?
>
> Listen, my dear brothers: Has not God chosen those who are poor in the eyes of the world to be rich in faith and to inherit the kingdom he promised those who love him? But you have insulted the poor (2:1–6).

Prejudice destroys faith. Faith destroys prejudice. The two cannot coexist in a church or an individual Christian.

I remember being invited to speak on the subject of racial violence at a state college campus during the 1960s. I pointed out that one of the tragic causes of the racial conflict in our land is the church of Jesus Christ. This statement shocked many people, for they expected that I, a pastor, would defend the record of the church in race relations. Instead, I went on to say

> Faith and prejudice cannot coexist in a church or an individual Christian.

> *If the church practices bias and discrimination, then prejudice takes root like a weed in the soil of our society.*

that if the church had been what it should have been, if Christians in both the North and the South actually received African-Americans and other minorities as fully equal brothers and sisters in Christ Jesus, this whole conflict would long since have disappeared.

The church has an enormous impact on attitudes in society. If the church practices bias and discrimination, then prejudice takes root like a weed in the soil of our society.

Deeds of Mercy

Second, faith is made visible by deeds of mercy. James was eminently practical, and he sets forth some eminently practical scenarios for us so that we can see his point with inescapable clarity:

> *What good is it, my brothers, if a man claims to have faith but has no deeds? Can such faith save him? Suppose a brother or sister is without clothes and daily food. If one of you says to him, "Go, I wish you well; keep warm and well fed," but does nothing about his physical needs, what good is it? In the same way, faith by itself, if it is not accompanied by action, is dead.*
> *But someone will say, "You have faith; I have deeds."*
> *Show me your faith without deeds, and I will show you my faith by what I do (2:14–18).*

Notice that James is not saying that we can be saved by good works. He is clearly saying that only faith, not works, can save us, but genuine faith is validated by action. What good is it if we tell a starving person, "I feel for you, and I'll pray for you," yet we do nothing to alleviate his hunger? That's not faith. That's just a pious display. Can you imagine Jesus treating someone that way? Real faith doesn't just talk, it acts. See Matthew 25:42–43.

Controlled Tongue

Next, James devotes all of chapter 3 to the third way by which faith is made visible and recognizable: a controlled tongue. He uses a series of vivid figures of speech to describe the tongue: It is "set on fire by hell." You can tame every beast and bird and reptile, but no one can control his or her tongue. The tongue, James says, is the member of our body most closely linked to our real nature. It shows what is motivating us, and, therefore, what you say reveals what you are. James

> *The tongue, James says, is the member of our body most closely linked to our real nature.*

wants us to understand that if we claim to be Christians and to have faith in Jesus Christ, our tongues must submit to His control.

This is not to suggest that Christians should never reprove or confront one another, but any confrontation of a brother or sister in Christ should be gentle, loving, and humble—not caustic, humiliating, and bitter. As Paul says in Ephesians, we are to speak the truth, but we are to speak the truth in love.

When Faith Fails

In chapter 4 and most of chapter 5, James answers the question, "What happens when faith fails? What if we fail to demonstrate our faith by the way we live and speak?" Answer: War breaks out. These wars and fights among Christian brothers and sisters are the result of prayerlessness, which is itself a demonstration of faithlessness. Faith is evidenced through prayer, and prayer produces love and peace. When faith fails, prayer fails; then fighting, arguments, hatred, and distrust break out. James writes: *Fighting, Arguments, Hatred, and Distrust*

> *You want something but don't get it. You kill and covet, but you cannot have what you want. You quarrel and fight. You do not have, because you do not ask God (4:2).*

That is the trouble! We fight with each other because we do not ask God for anything. We do not take from Him the nature of love and compassion He offers us. We choose not to receive from Him that sweetness of tongue that will turn away hostility and produce peace. Instead, we lash out and fight with one another.

The next thing is that the love of the world comes in and pollutes our relationship with God. James writes: *Enemies of God*

> *You adulterous people, don't you know that friendship with the world is hatred toward God? Anyone who chooses to be a friend of the world becomes an enemy of God (4:4).*

James also addresses the practical issue of the way we judge each other and speak about one another: *Judging Others*

> *Brothers, do not slander one another. Anyone who speaks against his brother or judges him speaks against the law and judges it.*

When you judge the law, you are not keeping it, but sitting in judgment on it (4:11).

People who criticize others have put themselves above the Word of God and have assumed God's role as judge. Instead of letting the Word judge themselves, they become the judges of others.

Being Presumptuous

Another result of lack of faith is being presumptuous about our plans and not allowing God to be sovereign over our lives and our future. James writes:

Listen, you who say, "Today or tomorrow we will go to this or that city, spend a year there, carry on business and make money" (4:13).

This is not to say that we should not make plans or set goals for our lives. Of course we should. But we should never become arrogant or presumptuous. We should never think we own our lives or that we control our own destinies.

A college student once said to me, "I don't need Christianity. I've got all it takes to live my life. I don't need any help from God."

"Oh?" I said. "Well, tell me, how do you keep your heart beating and your lungs functioning?"

"What do you mean?"

"Well," I said, "your heart is beating away and your diaphragm keeps moving up and down, forcing air in and out of your lungs. How do you do that?"

He seemed flustered. "I . . . I don't know. It just takes care of itself, I guess."

"No, it doesn't," I countered. "Nothing takes care of itself. Someone's operating the involuntary processes of your body, keeping you alive from moment to moment."

Then I told him the story of my friend who was back in Washington, D.C., during World War II. He wanted to fly from Washington to New York during those days when you needed a priority for air travel. So he went into the ticket office and said to the woman at the desk, "I want a ticket for New York."

"Do you have a priority?" she asked.

"I didn't know I needed one," he replied. "How do I get a priority?"

"Well," she said, "if you work for the government or for the airlines, I could give you one."

"I don't work for either of them," my friend replied. "But I'll tell you who I do work for. I work for the One who owns the air that your airline flies its planes through!"

She looked at him strangely. "Well, I don't think that's good enough to get you a priority."

He leaned over and said, "Did you ever think what would happen if my boss shut off your air for ten minutes?"

She blinked perplexedly, then said, "Just a minute, I'll see what I can do." She was gone for a few moments, then returned—with a priority in hand. "You can go right aboard," she said. She recognized that my friend served the highest authority of all!

Contrary to what many people seem to think, we are not the ultimate authority over our lives—God is. We should never become arrogant or presumptuous about our plans for the future. The more we respect His sovereignty over our lives, the better equipped we will be to adjust to the unforeseen circumstances that come our way. Time is in God's hands, not ours.

> We are not the ultimate authority over our lives—God is.

Christian Community

In chapter 5, James paints a beautiful word picture of authentic Christian community. This image of communion revolves around four qualities: confession, prayer, honesty, and love. James writes:

> *Confess your sins to each other and pray for each other so that you may be healed. The prayer of a righteous man is powerful and effective (5:16).*

Christian fellowship requires us to talk openly with trusted Christian brothers and sisters about our problems and to pray for each other for insight and healing of those problems. True Christian intimacy takes place as we come out from behind our masks, as we quit trying to be something we are not and simply become what we really are. As we confess our faults and pain with each other and pray for one another, we live out the honesty and truth of God. Immediately, the grace of the God of truth, the God who loves truth, will flow through us—individually and as a family of faith. We will become a true community, and the world will press its nose against the glass, trying to get what we have, trying to become what we are.

I am convinced that this is the missing element in society today: genuine *Koinonia* fellowship and community, what the Greek New Testament calls *koinonia*. It is missing even in many (if not most) of our churches, where we have a lot of Christians living in little isolation cells not willing to let anyone into their lives, not willing to let anyone see who they truly are. You ask them how things are going, and they respond automatically, "Oh, great!" But they are not great at all, and this kind of hypocrisy must end. James says that God will be in your midst if you take down the fences, join hands with other Christians, pray together, and be honest with one another.

In and through and around and above and below it all, binding our community together, must be genuine Christlike love, expressed in an intense concern and caring for one another—a concern that dares to tell the truth to one another and that will not let a brother or sister go. The closing verses of James give us the pattern:

> *My brothers, if one of you should wander from the truth and someone should bring him back, remember this: Whoever turns a sinner from the error of his way will save him from death and cover over a multitude of sins (5:19–20).*

Here we have a wonderful glimpse into the life of the early church and into the church as it should be today. No wonder these Christians turned the city of Jerusalem upside down! Under the leadership of this man, James the Just, the church grew until there was a vast multitude of believers who lived by mutual confession, prayer, honesty, and love. The world today aches for Christians who will return to this pattern, who will become a genuine *koinonia* community, a family of faith, modeling the character of Christ.

That is the claim of the Christian faith upon our lives. That is the call of this gospel we claim to believe in. That is the message of the epistle of James to you and me today. If we truly believe it, let's live it! And let's turn the world upside down for Jesus once more!

NOTES

NOTES

NOTES

CHAPTER FOUR

1 PETER: LIVING STONES

I N JULY OF THE YEAR A.D. 64, a great fire broke out in the city of Rome. Soon, the entire city was engulfed in flames. Hundreds of public buildings burned to the ground, thousands of houses were destroyed, and most of the city's inhabitants were left homeless. History concludes that Emperor Nero set that fire to destroy the ramshackle buildings of Rome and make room to erect marble palaces and other monuments to his name. This event gave rise to the saying, "Nero fiddled while Rome burned," even though the violin had not yet been invented. Historians of the time claim that Emperor Nero was seen looking over the city and enjoying the fire.

The Context of
1 Peter: The
Persecutions
under Nero

The people were incensed to the point of revolution, so Nero created a scapegoat to blame for the fire: a group of people called Christians. These Christians followed a man named Christ, about whom strange things were said. He had supposedly been crucified, then was raised to life again. There were wild rumors about the strange practices of His followers. These Christians were considered cannibals because they talked about meeting in houses and drinking the blood and eating the body of their Master. They spoke about "agape-love feasts," where they greeted one another with a holy kiss and shared their innermost problems with each other. These stories became the basis for rumors of wild sex orgies. Christians were already subject to suspicion, so when Nero blamed them for the burning of Rome, the people of Rome believed him.

With the people's support, Nero initiated a series of persecutions against the Christians. Christians were dipped in tar and burned alive as torches to light the emperor's gardens when he threw an outdoor party. They were tied to chariots and dragged through the streets of Rome until dead. They were thrown to the lions. They were sealed up in leather bags and thrown into water so that when the leather bags shrank, the Christians inside were squeezed and suffocated to death. In a hundred other cruelly inventive ways, Nero exploited satanically inspired hatred against Christians and used them to satiate his own sadistic lusts.

This time of unbelievably harsh persecution of Christians in Rome was the context for the epistle of 1 Peter.

This time of unbelievably harsh persecution of Christians in Rome was the context for the epistle of 1 Peter.

A Letter for Trials and Pressures

Most Bible scholars believe that Peter wrote his first letter from the city of Rome. He begins with these words:

Peter, an apostle of Jesus Christ,
To God's elect, strangers in the world, scattered throughout
Pontus, Galatia, Cappadocia, Asia and Bithynia, who have been
chosen according to the foreknowledge of God the Father, through
the sanctifying work of the Spirit, for obedience to Jesus Christ and
sprinkling by his blood:
Grace and peace be yours in abundance (1:1–2).

Later in this epistle, Peter writes:

She who is in Babylon, chosen together with you, sends you her
greetings, and so does my son Mark (5:13).

Peter was not talking about the ancient city of Babylon on the Euphrates River. Most scholars agree that Peter was undoubtedly using the term that was common among first-century Christians. They often referred to Rome as "Babylon" because the idolatry, blood lust, and open immorality of ancient Babylon had infected the capital of the Roman Empire. His greeting from "she who is in Babylon" suggests that Peter himself was in Babylon—or Rome—at the time.

Peter probably wrote this letter from the city of Rome in about A.D. 67. He addressed it to Christians scattered about the cities of the northeast province of Asia Minor (present-day Turkey). They were being hounded and persecuted all through the empire because of Nero's proclamation against them, so the apostle Peter wrote to encourage them and embolden them to face the deadly persecution of the Roman state.

This letter is especially helpful to anyone undergoing trial or suffering of any kind. If you wonder what God is doing in the world and how to withstand the pressures and pain, become intimately acquainted with 1 Peter.

The Outline of 1 Peter

Here is an outline of Peter's first letter:

Our Salvation as Believers (1 Peter 1:1–2:12)

1. Peter's greeting — 1:1–2
2. Salvation: Our hope for times of trial — 1:3–12

3. Sanctification: Living out our hope	1:13–2:12
A. Be holy	1:13–21
B. Love one another	1:22–25
C. Desire the pure milk of the Word	2:1–10
D. Abstain from sinful lusts	2:11–12

Our Submission as Believers (1 Peter 2:13–3:12)

4. Submission to ruling authorities	2:13–17
5. Submission in business matters	2:18–25
6. Submission in the marriage relationship	3:1–7
7. Submission in all areas of the Christian life	3:8–12

Our Suffering as Believers (1 Peter 3:13–5:14)

8. How to endure suffering patiently	3:13–17
9. The example of Jesus Christ	3:18–4:6
10. More instruction in how to endure suffering	4:7–19
11. How to minister through suffering (instructions to elders and to the saints)	5:1–9
12. Conclusion and benediction	5:10–14

A Living Hope

This letter begins with the greatest fact in the life of any Christian: our relationship to Jesus Christ through the miracle of the new birth:

> *Praise be to the God and Father of our Lord Jesus Christ! In his great mercy he has given us new birth (1:3).*

As a boy, I would hear Christians give their testimonies. They would say, "The greatest thing that ever happened to me was the day I met Jesus Christ." Well, I was a Christian, but deep down in my heart, I didn't really believe it was the greatest thing that had ever happened to me. In fact, it seemed to be a rather minor incident in my life. I didn't have a shattering emotional experience at my conversion. The windows of heaven didn't open up and flood my soul with light. I was ten years old when I asked Jesus into my life, and though it was a precious experience and one I did not discount, it didn't compare to some of the other experiences and important decisions of my life.

But now as I look back over the decades of my Christian life, I can say that beyond a shadow of a doubt that decision was the greatest decision of my life. Everything else that has happened to me has been related to that one turning point in my life at age ten.

The reason that the experience of the new birth is so important is not only that we have a hope of heaven when we die but that we also have a living hope to carry us through this life. What an important word for us in this hopeless age! Peter writes:

> *In his great mercy he has given us new birth into a living hope through the resurrection of Jesus Christ from the dead, and into an inheritance that can never perish, spoil or fade—kept in heaven for you, who through faith are shielded by God's power until the coming of the salvation that is ready to be revealed in the last time (1:3–5).*

Here is an expression of the hope of heaven, a place in eternity that is already reserved for us. But that is not all. Peter says that we not only have a living hope for the future and eternity, but we have present power—right now, today! We are kept and sustained by that power, guarded through faith for a salvation that is ready to be revealed.

> Peter says that we not only have a living hope for the future and eternity, but we have present power—right now, today!

A Rejoicing Love

Peter also reminds us of another benefit that we enjoy because we have received Jesus as Lord and Savior, a benefit that can carry us through times of trial—a rejoicing love:

> *Though you have not seen him, you love him; and even though you do not see him now, you believe in him and are filled with an inexpressible and glorious joy (1:8).*

I hope you know what Peter is talking about, the kind of quiet joy that fills your heart simply because you know Jesus in an intimate, personal way. This joy is not the result of anything He does for you but simply the result of who He is and of the fact that He loves you and you love Him. Even though you cannot see Him you love Him.

Peter goes on to say that the plan of salvation has been predicted by the Old Testament prophets. Peter writes:

Concerning this salvation, the prophets, who spoke of the grace that was to come to you, searched intently and with the greatest care, trying to find out the time and circumstances to which the Spirit of Christ in them was pointing when he predicted the sufferings of Christ and the glories that would follow (1:10–11).

This is not some new invention or wild fable. The birth, life, death, and resurrection of Jesus Christ—which is our hope of salvation—was planned since the beginning of time and was predicted throughout the Old Testament.

The Three Marks of a Genuine Christian

Be Holy

Peter sets forth three marks as distinctives that every Christian should bear.

First mark: "Be holy" (see 1 Peter 1:14–16). What do you think of when you hear that word holy? Do you think of someone who has been stewed in vinegar? Someone so piously sour that he or she is always mouthing righteous-sounding words, speaking a super-religious language? Is this what holiness means to you? If so, then you have missed the biblical meaning of the command to "be holy."

The Old Testament talks about "the beauty of holiness." Obviously, a sour-pickle personality is not what you would call "the beauty of holiness." A truly holy person is a person with an attractive, beautiful personality. At base, the word *holiness* means "wholeness." A holy person is a whole person. Holy people are whole-minded, whole-hearted, and whole-spirited. They are dedicated to God, committed to loving, accepting, and forgiving others, and focused on living righteously and joyfully. They have the healthiest personalities you can imagine. Their talk is godly, and their lifestyle mirrors their talk. There is no conflict between their words and their walk. They are at rest. They are adjusted. They are content because their trust is in God. That's what holiness truly is.

> A holy person is a whole person.

I love holy people. I wish we were all holy in the church; it would be so much fun going to church! When churches experience fights, splits, and discord, it is because God's people are not living holy lives.

Be Reverently Fearful

Second mark: Be reverently fearful (see 1 Peter 1:17–19). Peter says, "Be fearful." Fearful? Yes, God does indeed want us to be fearful, but that word fearful needs some explanation. Peter is not saying we should be timid or terrorized or paralyzed with dread. Rather, Peter challenges us toward what he calls reverent fear:

> *Since you call on a Father who judges each man's work impartially, live your lives as strangers here in reverent fear. For you know that it was not with perishable things such as silver or gold that you were redeemed from the empty way of life handed down to you from your forefathers, but with the precious blood of Christ, a lamb without blemish or defect (1:17–19).*

The kind of fear that Peter describes is really an honest and profound respect for God. Peter says, in effect, "Remember whom you are dealing with. You are not dealing with another human being who can be fooled by your actions and attitudes. You are dealing with one who knows you better than you know yourself. He is no respecter of persons. So conduct yourself with fear, awe, and respect for the eternal, omnipotent, all-knowing God of the universe. Be honest with God and with yourself, remembering that you are not your own, you have been bought with the precious blood of Jesus Christ."

Third mark: "Be priests" (see 1 Peter 2:4–5). The apostle writes:

A Royal Priest

> *As you come to him, the living Stone—rejected by men but chosen by God and precious to him—you also, like living stones, are being built into a spiritual house to be a holy priesthood, offering spiritual sacrifices acceptable to God through Jesus Christ.*

Here is the answer to a question people often ask: "What did Jesus mean when He said to this apostle, 'I tell you that you are Peter, and on this rock I will build my church'?" (Matthew 16:18). We know that the name Peter means "rock," and the Roman Catholic Church tells us that Jesus meant He was going to build His church upon Peter. But Peter says no. He was there, and He ought to know. He says, "Jesus is the rock." And every believer who comes to Christ is like a stone built upon that Rock, that great underlying Rock upon which God is erecting the institution called the church.

What is the goal of building us up as stones upon the Rock? He is building us up as a priesthood, as a people dedicated and offered to God, special and holy. Peter writes:

You are a chosen people, a royal priesthood, a holy nation, a people belonging to God, that you may declare the praises of him who called you out of darkness into his wonderful light (2:9).

> God wants us to declare to the world what He has done for us.

That is what God wants: He wants us to declare to the world what He has done for us. As we do so, we offer to God a sweet-smelling offering and a savor of worship to Him. So these are the three distinctives Peter says should mark the life of every Christian: Be holy. Be reverently fearful. And be a priesthood, set apart to God.

Practical Advice

Peter then deals with the more practical aspects of life, with how we should live our lives, whether as citizens of the Roman Empire or of the United States of America. Though they lived under persecution, the first-century Christians still had certain obligations. Today, many of us see our own government behaving in ways we disapprove of, ways we feel are unrighteous and even harmful to us, yet we still have certain obligations as citizens. Peter writes:

Dear friends, I urge you, as aliens and strangers in the world, to abstain from sinful desires, which war against your soul. Live such good lives among the pagans that, though they accuse you of doing wrong, they may see your good deeds and glorify God on the day he visits us.

Submit yourselves for the Lord's sake to every authority instituted among men: whether to the king, as the supreme authority, or to governors, who are sent by him to punish those who do wrong and to commend those who do right. For it is God's will that by doing good you should silence the ignorant talk of foolish men. Live as free men, but do not use your freedom as a cover-up for evil; live as servants of God. Show proper respect to everyone: Love the brotherhood of believers, fear God, honor the king (2:11–17).

Honor the king? But the king Peter refers to is Nero! He is the one who drags Christians behind his chariot and burns them as living torches in his garden! Honor *him*? Surely, Peter must be out of his mind! Yet that is God's word to us: As citizens, we owe honor to those in authority over us.

Then Peter talks about servants:

> *Slaves, submit yourselves to your masters with all respect, not only to those who are good and considerate, but also to those who are harsh. For it is commendable if a man bears up under the pain of unjust suffering because he is conscious of God. But how is it to your credit if you receive a beating for doing wrong and endure it? But if you suffer for doing good and you endure it, this is commendable before God. To this you were called, because Christ suffered for you, leaving you an example, that you should follow in his steps.*
> *"He committed no sin, and no deceit was found in his mouth"* (2:18–22).

So servants are to obey and respect their masters, and I might add that the principle is clear that employees are to obey and respect their employers. If an employer or master is unjust, we are not to behave unjustly in return. We do not return insult for insult. We commit ourselves to the Lord.

Next, Peter moves into the Christian home, encouraging Christians to honor one another and behave justly and considerately (3:1–7).

Then he addresses the entire church, encouraging the family of faith to live together in unity, loving one another as brothers and sisters, behaving tenderly and humbly with one another. This is the mark of our Christian fellowship and community (3:8–14).

Peter tells us to always be ready to share the good news of Jesus Christ with those around us. He writes:

> *In your hearts set apart Christ as Lord. Always be prepared to give an answer to everyone who asks you to give the reason for the hope that you have. But do this with gentleness and respect, keeping a clear conscience, so that those who speak maliciously against your good behavior in Christ may be ashamed of their slander (3:15–16).*

Notice that Peter expects Christians to live such positive, hopeful, exemplary lives that people will be eager to know why. He says, in effect, "When people ask you why you're such an optimistic, cheerful, righteous person, have an answer ready for them. Be prepared to tell them that Jesus is the answer." Saint Francis of Assisi understood this principle well; he always taught his disciples that they should spread the gospel through the way they lived and loved. "Preach the gospel at all times," Saint Francis advised. "If necessary, use words."

A Difficult Passage

Then comes a difficult passage about spirits in prison and baptism—passages many Christians have struggled with. But the key to 1 Peter 3 is verse 18:

> *Christ died for sins once for all, the righteous for the unrighteous, to bring you to God. He was put to death in the body but made alive by the Spirit.*

Jesus suffered in order to bring us to God. He came in the flesh, and He died in the flesh. He did all this that He might accomplish the great goal of God's plan: bringing us to God.

Peter recalls the way the gospel was preached in Noah's day and how the Spirit of Christ, speaking through Noah, preached to the people so that he might bring them to God. But they refused to believe Noah, and the ark becomes a symbol of the life of the Lord Jesus Christ, carrying us over the floods of judgment and bringing us to God. Baptism, which is also a picture that relates to the ark, saves us just as the ark saved Noah. Baptism is that which now saves us, but Peter is very clear at this point that he is not talking about water baptism:

> *This water [the water of the Genesis flood] symbolizes baptism [the baptism of the Holy Spirit] that now saves you also—not the removal of dirt from the body [which is what water baptism accomplishes] but the pledge of a good conscience toward God [which is accomplished by salvation]. It saves you by the resurrection of Jesus Christ (3:21).*

> The baptism of the Spirit occurs at the moment of salvation.

The baptism of the Spirit occurs at the moment of salvation and puts us into the ark of safety, our Lord Jesus. Water baptism is the visible symbol of the real baptism that saves us, the baptism of the Holy Spirit. Salvation removes the stain of guilt and sin from our lives, replacing it with a clear conscience through the resurrection of Jesus Christ. If you read the passage in that light, I believe you will have no difficulty with it.

Return Good for Evil

Peter then concludes his discussion of the issue of suffering, encouraging us as Christians to remember that we are not to live as the worldly, the Gentiles, who return evil for evil. Rather, we are to return good for evil. We are not to be concerned about our own satisfaction and our own rights. We are to be concerned about living after the pattern of Jesus Christ, the suffering servant. When we begin to insist on our rights, even in small ways, we nullify our witness. We cease to resemble Christ.

A young boy once became very concerned about all the chores he had to do around the house. He began to feel exploited, so he decided to demand his rights. He did this by presenting a bill for all the chores he had done:

Mowing the lawn	$1.00
Making my bed	.50
Vacuuming the rug	.50
Pulling weeds	1.00
Taking out the garbage	.50
Cleaning up after the dog	.50
Washing the dishes	1.00
	$5.00

The next morning, the boy placed the bill beside his mother's breakfast plate. She read it, but she did not say anything. The next morning he found a list beside his plate. It read:

Washing your clothes	no charge
Fixing your meals	no charge
Providing shelter	no charge
Driving you to soccer and baseball practice	no charge
Helping you with your homework	no charge
Trip to Disneyland	no charge
Teaching you right from wrong, and telling you about Jesus	
Etc., etc., etc.	no charge
	Absolutely no charge, done out of love

The boy read it, and then he hugged his mom and did all his chores without complaint.

We are to do what this mother did—return good for evil. She could have lectured the boy on his ingratitude and selfishness. Instead, she showed him how much she loved him, and he responded to that love.

The End of All Things

The closing section of the letter deals with life in the church, the body of Christ. Peter writes:

> The end of all things is near. Therefore be clear minded and self-controlled so that you can pray. Above all, love each other deeply, because love covers over a multitude of sins. Offer hospitality to one another without grumbling. Each one should use whatever gift he has received to serve others, faithfully administering God's grace in its various forms. If anyone speaks, he should do it as one speaking the very words of God. If anyone serves, he should do it with the strength God provides, so that in all things God may be praised through Jesus Christ. To him be the glory and the power for ever and ever. Amen (4:7–11).

As the end draws near and the world slouches toward Armageddon, He expects His church to stand in shining contrast to the world's darkness.

Here is the Lord's program for the end of the age, and He plans to carry it out through you and me in the church. As the end draws near and the world slouches toward Armageddon, He expects His church to stand in stark, shining contrast to the world's darkness. He intends our lives, both individually and as a body, to be characterized by agape love so wide and so deep that it covers any sin or wrong that is done to us; by generosity and gracious hospitality toward our brothers and sisters in Christ; by the exercise of our spiritual gifts so that we can show God's grace to one another and to the world; by speaking truthfully and gently to one another; by serving one another to the greatest degree, so that Jesus will be exemplified and God will be praised and glorified. This is God's plan. It may not look like a very impressive plan in the eyes of the world, but in the eyes of heaven, this is a powerful plan that will accomplish the will of God.

Peter goes on, in 4:12–19, to speak of suffering as a privilege, because we have an opportunity to share Christ's sufferings—not suffering as wrong-doers but rejoicing in the fact that God is at work through our suffering.

In chapter 5, Peter then speaks of the mutual ministry of the elders to the members and of the members one to another. Then he returns one final time to the matter of suffering in verse 10:

> *The God of all grace, who called you to his eternal glory in Christ, after you have suffered a little while, will himself restore you and make you strong, firm and steadfast.*

This present suffering is just for a little while, then Christ himself will restore us to strength and health—a strength that can never fail, a vitality that can never fade—reserved for us in heaven. The world is temporal, more temporal than we human beings are. God will bring an end to the world, but we will go on forever with Him. This is God's plan.

As we see the end approaching, as we suffer and endure for Jesus' sake, the words of 1 Peter are a blessing and a comfort. "Peace to all of you who are in Christ," Peter says in the very last line of his letter. Amid our trials and sufferings, amid a world that is crumbling all around us—peace! That is the encouraging message of 1 Peter.

God will bring an end to the world, but we will go on forever with Him.

NOTES

NOTES

NOTES

NOTES

CHAPTER FIVE

2 PETER:
FAITH *in the* FACE
of FALSEHOOD

I T ALMOST SEEMS THAT 2 PETER was written to us at this crucial time, in the twenty-first century. Every word of this book is so pertinent, so contemporary, and so full of practical advice for today, that it confirms two truths:

1. The Bible is relevant, fresh, and vital; it never goes out of date.

2. History has come full circle; we live in days very similar to those of the first century, and we face conditions similar to the ones faced by the early church.

Whereas the theme of 1 Peter was how to rejoice in the face of suffering, the theme of 2 Peter is how to maintain faith in the face of falsehood—how to detect error, how to avoid the lure of deception, how to know and do what is right in a world gone wrong.

The Outline of 2 Peter

Second Peter can be outlined neatly. Each of its three chapters portrays a different facet of the main theme. Here is an overview of the letter:

What the Christian Life Is All About (2 Peter 1)

1.	Peter's greeting	1:1–2
2.	How we grow in Christ	1:3–14
3.	The basis of our faith	1:15–21

Warning against False Teachers (2 Peter 2)

4.	The danger of false teachers	2:1–3
5.	The destruction of false teachers	2:4–9
6.	The description of false teachers	2:10–22

The Certainty of Our Lord's Return (2 Peter 3)

7.	Scoffers in the last days	3:1–7
8.	The arrival of the day of the Lord	3:8–10
9.	How to live in expectation of His return	3:11–18

It's a simple outline for a very practical letter, just as you might expect from a practical, hardheaded Christian like Peter.

Mighty Apostles or Ordinary Believers

This letter was probably written from Rome, as was 1 Peter. In fact, Peter may have been a prisoner of Emperor Nero. From this letter we know that Peter is, at the very least, in great danger.

Peter says that he feels the time is drawing near when he is to put off his body—what he refers to as his tent, his habitation—to go and be with the Lord. He says the Lord himself showed him this, as recorded for us at the close of the gospel of John. In John 21:18, Jesus had told Peter that a time would come when someone would bind his hands and lead him where he did not want to go. Peter understood this to mean that he was to suffer and die as our Lord died, on a cross. Tradition tells us Peter was indeed crucified and that he was so humbled by the fact that he was counted worthy to die the same death as his Lord that he begged his captors to crucify him upside down.

Peter opens his second letter with these words:

> *Simon Peter, a servant and apostle of Jesus Christ,*
>   *To those who through the righteousness of our God and Savior Jesus Christ have received a faith as precious as ours:*
>   *Grace and peace be yours in abundance through the knowledge of God and of Jesus our Lord (2 Peter 1:1–2).*

Note that phrase: "To those who . . . have received a faith as precious as ours." Think of that! Christians today are tempted to think of the apostles as mighty men of sterling character and superhuman faith. Notice, however, that the apostles never thought of themselves that way. Truly, the weakest believer holds in his or her hands all that the mightiest saint ever possessed. That is the theme of Peter's opening chapter. Listen to these words:

> The weakest believer enjoys all that the mightiest saint ever possessed.

> *His divine power has given us everything we need for life and godliness through our knowledge of him who called us by his own glory and goodness (1:3).*

All of us who have genuinely come to Jesus Christ—without exception—have everything we need to handle life and to manifest godliness (which literally means "God-likeness").

Do you understand and truly believe that this statement by Peter applies to your life right now? A lot of people do not. They are always looking for something more—some new experience, some transforming new truth, some further revelation, some elevating emotional high—and they think that without these things they can never be the kind of Christians they ought to be.

Peter says, in effect, "You don't need any new experience or revelation. You already have all you need to be spiritually empowered and energized to serve God, please God, and imitate God in your lifestyle. If you have come to Christ, you have all there is to have of Him, and you have all He has to give you. You have all power and all things that pertain to life and godliness though the knowledge of Him. If something is missing, it's not because you need any more of Christ. It may be that Christ needs more of you. You simply need to turn more of your life and your will over to Him."

> If something is missing, it's not because you need any more of Christ; it may be that Christ needs more of you.

Two Channels of God's Power

If what Peter says is true (and it is), then we have no excuse for failure. If we have everything in Christ, we need only to know more of Him and to yield more to Him, and our problems will be solved. To me, the great thing about being a Christian is that in Jesus Christ I really am finding practical answers to every problem that confronts me.

Obviously, coming to Christ does not automatically enable us to know everything. But we do gain insight and understanding to handle the difficulties, heartaches, and problems of life. We do gain the power to live godly, Christlike lives. God's power is already granted to us, and it comes to us through two channels: (1) His promises, and (2) putting our faith into practice.

His Promises   First, the promises. Peter writes:

> *Through these he has given us his very great and precious promises, so that through them you may participate in the divine nature and escape the corruption in the world caused by evil desires (1:4).*

These are not just glowing words, not just so much theological twaddle. These are sure guarantees that God has given us, and He will honor them with all His power and authority as the Creator-God of the universe. His nature and His character are at stake in these words.

So the first thing we need to do is to learn what He has promised, and that means we must acquaint ourselves with those promises, as contained in the Scriptures. You cannot possibly find fulfillment and victory in your life and really discover the kind of person God wants you to be unless you study and understand God's Word.

As we come to know and rely on God's promises, we become strengthened and empowered to "escape the corruption in the world caused by evil desires." So much evil and corruption surround us. Our airwaves, the Internet, cable TV, radio, books, magazines, and even our workplaces and social arenas are polluted by the evil of this world. We see sexual corruption, greed, materialism, ambition, pride, and selfishness. You cannot escape from such pervasive corruption unless you have armored yourself in the truth of God.

The second means of receiving God's power for our lives is found in 1:5–7:   Our Practice

> For this very reason, make every effort to add to your faith goodness; and to goodness, knowledge; and to knowledge, self-control; and to self-control, perseverance; and to perseverance, godliness; and to godliness, brotherly kindness; and to brotherly kindness, love.

In other words, once you have faith, you must put it into practice. You must begin growing and applying your faith, from moment to moment, from deed to deed, one day at a time. Whenever you identify a new area of your life that needs to be dealt with—a problem with anger, a lack of self-control, harshness in dealing with others, a timidity and lack of perseverance—then you work to bring that area of your life in line with your faith. It's important to understand that faith is not an event; it's a process. As we grow and mature in Christ, He gradually opens our eyes to different aspects of our characters that are not under His control. As we make ourselves available to Him in obedience, He gradually chips away at our imperfections, helping us to become more and more like His own perfect character.

Faith is not an event; it's a process.

And what is the result of putting our faith into practice on a daily basis? Peter writes:

> If you possess these qualities in increasing measure, they will keep you from being ineffective and unproductive in your knowledge of our Lord Jesus Christ (1:8).

A recipe for success as a Christian is right here in this passage: faith and obedience. Knowledge of God's promises coupled with the willingness to apply those promises in the specific situations of life is what enables

Christians to be effective. And what of those who do not know and apply God's promises? Peter replies:

> *If anyone does not have them, he is nearsighted and blind, and has forgotten that he has been cleansed from his past sins (1:9).*

Christians who fail to live according to their faith are blind. Their conversion experiences seem to have little or no effect on them. They leave themselves open for doubt, backsliding, and even self-destruction through sin. Therefore, writes Peter in verses 10–11:

> *Be all the more eager to make your calling and election sure. For if you do these things, you will never fall, and you will receive a rich welcome into the eternal kingdom of our Lord and Savior Jesus Christ.*

When the Lord calls you home, the trumpets will blare in glory at your entrance into the kingdom because you have found the secret of successful living, and you have been effective in your service to God.

Two Guarantees

Peter reveals two guarantees that support the faith he commends to us: (1) his own eyewitness account of the life of the Lord Jesus Christ, and (2) the voice of the Old Testament prophets. He writes:

> *We did not follow cleverly invented stories when we told you about the power and coming of our Lord Jesus Christ, but we were eyewitnesses of his majesty. For he received honor and glory from God the Father when the voice came to him from the Majestic Glory, saying, "This is my Son, whom I love; with him I am well pleased." We ourselves heard this voice that came from heaven when we were with him on the sacred mountain (1:16–18).*

Eyewitness Accounts

Peter refers to the event cited in Matthew 17 and Mark 9, where Jesus was transfigured on the mountain, when His face shone and His clothes became as white as light. Peter says, "We were eyewitnesses of his majesty." And that is where Christian faith rests: on the credible eyewitness accounts of men and women who were there and who simply reported what they saw and heard Jesus do.

Peter goes on to state the second guarantee. Our faith is confirmed, Old Testament
he says, by another voice—the voice of the Old Testament prophets. Prophets
He writes:

> We have the word of the prophets made more certain, and you will
> do well to pay attention to it, as to a light shining in a dark place,
> until the day dawns and the morning star rises in your hearts.
> Above all, you must understand that no prophecy of Scripture came
> about by the prophet's own interpretation. For prophecy never had
> its origin in the will of man, but men spoke from God as they were
> carried along by the Holy Spirit (1:19–21).

These men did not write their own opinions. They wrote under instruction from the Spirit of God, and they accurately predicted events that were to occur centuries later. Two guarantees—eyewitnesses and fulfilled prophecy—support our faith.

A Warning against False Teachers

In chapter 2, Peter sounds a warning against false teachers, and his words are as relevant today as they were when the ink was still wet on the page:

> There were also false prophets among the people, just as there will
> be false teachers among you. They will secretly introduce destructive
> heresies, even denying the sovereign Lord who bought them—bringing
> swift destruction on themselves. Many will follow their shameful ways
> and will bring the way of truth into disrepute (2:1–2).

Today we see these words fulfilled in many ways. We have seen cults in which the leaders claim to be Jesus Christ and in which members have sometimes been destroyed through horrible mass suicides. Those are extreme cases. But there are also more subtle cases where false teachers introduce destructive heresies into individual churches—or even into entire denominations.

Notice that Peter says, "They will secretly introduce destructive heresies, even denying the sovereign Lord who bought them," which tells us that these false teachers are not mere atheistic antago.

These teachers claim to h⁻
Christians and pr⁻ᶠ
love the L
their teachι
everything h.

Christianity. These teachers claim to be Christians and profess to love the Lord Jesus, yet their teachings actually deny everything He stood for!

As a result of these false teachers, says Peter, the truth of the gospel will be brought into disrepute. People will look down on those who believe the Bible; they will consider believers simple-minded, ignorant folk from the Dark Ages, or worse—narrow-minded bigots.

In 2:3–9, Peter assures us that God will surely judge these false teachers just as He dealt with the rebellious angels, just as He dealt with the sinners of the ancient world whom He judged with a flood, and just as He dealt with the sinful cities of Sodom and Gomorrah. Peter says that the godly will be rescued from trial, just as Noah was saved from the flood and Lot was saved from the destruction of Sodom.

False Teachers Described

In verses 10–22, Peter gives a vivid description of the characteristics of these false teachers. They are:

- presumptuous; eloquent with impressive words about issues of life, salvation, and spirituality, but actually ignorant of God's truth
- like animals, creatures of instinct; reviling matters about which they are ignorant
- shameless; they encourage licentiousness and sexual misconduct
- greedy; for the sake of money, they will teach anything people want to hear
- boastful and full of folly
- slaves of corruption, even while they promise freedom (much like those today who advocate drug abuse and sexual depravity)
- aware of what the Scriptures say, yet deny their truth and power, choosing instead to follow their own delusions

Encouragement for the Last Days

In chapter 3, Peter encourages us not to be discouraged by this prevailing atmosphere of error. Remember that Jesus is return-ing, and He will set matters right. Even though the scoffers and false teachers may say that the universe is stable and unchanging, never affected or invaded by divine power, we know that the universe is actually temporary and passing away. God has intervened in the past and will intervene in the future. The flood of Genesis occurred in the past, but it points to a day in the future when the world will be

> God has intervened in the past and will ene in the future.

destroyed again—not by water, but by fire. In verse 10, Peter writes:

The day of the Lord will come like a thief. The heavens will disappear with a roar; the elements will be destroyed by fire, and the earth and everything in it will be laid bare.

It may well be that the vivid description Peter sets down in this verse suggests the awful power of nuclear devastation or of an asteroid or comet collision with the earth. All that keeps life functioning on our world at all is the Word of God, the authority of God, and the will of God. All He needs to do is to alter some aspect of our physical universe and the whole mechanism of the universe collapses.

> All that keeps life functioning in our world at all is the Word of God, the authority of God, and the will of God.

Many of us look around at all the evil of the world, and we get impatient. We wonder why the Lord doesn't come and clean house right now. Why does He delay? We need to remember that a day with the Lord is as a thousand years, and a thousand years is as a day. Our concept of time is not the same as His. We also need to remember that God has a purpose in delaying, for which we ought to be grateful. Once God's judgment commences, it can't be stopped. He waits to give men and women a chance to think things through and reconsider their ways. He delays judgment in order to give us all a chance to repent.

Peter then confronts us with a searching question:

Since everything will be destroyed in this way, what kind of people ought you to be? (3:11).

Peter's own answer to that question is clear:

You ought to live holy and godly lives as you look forward to the day of God and speed its coming. That day will bring about the destruction of the heavens by fire, and the elements will melt in the heat (3:11–12).

Three Means of Hastening the Lord's Coming

Notice that Peter says that as we live holy, godly lives, we not expectantly for the day of God, we actually *speed its coming*. How hasten the coming of the Lord Jesus Christ? How do we help bring the end of global evil and help God to realize the hope that humankind has dreamed of for centuries—a world at peace, a world of plenty, a world of blessing and joy? In three ways:

Our prayers. Remember what the Lord Jesus taught us to pray? "Our Father in heaven, hallowed be your name, *your kingdom come*" (Matthew 6:9–10, italics added). That is a prayer for hastening the day of God. Remember John's prayer at the end of the book of Revelation? "Come, Lord Jesus" (Revelation 22:20). We are to pray for the end of this world system and the coming of the Lord's kingdom on earth, because that is the only way this world's ills and suffering will ever be ended.

Our witnessing. The gospel of the kingdom must be preached to all the nations, and then the end will come, says the Lord Jesus in Matthew 24:14. Whenever we share the good news of Jesus Christ with one other person, we bring the return of Jesus Christ a little bit closer.

> Whenever we share the good news of Jesus Christ with one other person, we bring the return of Jesus Christ a little bit closer.

Our obedience. The Jews say that if all of Israel would obey the law fully for one day, the Messiah would come. God is looking for men and women who will be obedient, who will truly be His. The only freedom we have is the freedom to serve either God or the devil. There is no middle ground, no third alternative. The "freedom" offered by sin and Satan ultimately leads to despair and enslavement. But the *genuine* freedom that comes with being a slave to Christ leads to *abundant* life and *eternal* life.

So, in view of the approaching return of Jesus Christ and the approaching end of this corrupt world system, Peter concludes, "make every effort to be found spotless, blameless and at peace with him" (2 Peter 3:14).

In a final postscript, verses 15 and 16, Peter says that Paul agrees that prayerful, obedient waiting for the Lord's return means salvation when the day of God appears—not eternal salvation, but being ready, not being caught unaware and unprepared when the dire end-of-the-world events begin to take place. When the rest of the world trembles with fear and despair, we who have prayed and worked to hasten that day will stand, expectant and unafraid.

Peter adds another warning against false teaching, this time in regard to those who twist and distort Paul's teachings, just as they do the other Scriptures. Do not listen to them, Peter warns. Don't be fooled.

Final Words of Warning, Blessing, and Encouragement

The final two verses include a final warning—and a final blessing and encouragement:

> *Dear friends, since you already know this, be on your guard so that you may not be carried away by the error of lawless men and fall from your secure position. But grow in the grace and knowledge of our Lord and Savior Jesus Christ. To him be glory both now and forever! Amen (3:17–18).*

We have all the facts we need for faith and for defending ourselves against falsehood. We have the unchangeable truth of Jesus Christ. Let's be on our guard so that we are not carried away or undermined by the false teachers who want to steal our faith. Though our faith is under attack, though truth is continually on the scaffold, we have the victory in hand. The Lord is coming soon, and we are praying, witnessing, and obeying Him in order to hasten that day. Amen! Come, Lord Jesus!

NOTES

NOTES

NOTES

NOTES

CHAPTER SIX

1 JOHN: AUTHENTIC CHRISTIANITY

JESUS HAD TWO DISCIPLES whom I particularly wish I could have known. One is Peter, the other is John. I love to read about these two. They are very different from each other in character and personality, yet both were close to Jesus Christ. Simon Peter was erratic, impulsive, and brash. Whenever he entered the scene, it was with a crash and a thud. Yet the Lord chose to make him a steady, stable, dependable "rock" (which is what his name, Peter, literally means). He became a rallying point for first-century Christians in those days of intense persecution.

John was another disciple who was dramatically transformed by his encounter with Jesus Christ. He was a young man when he began following Christ. In fact, many Bible scholars believe he was a teen-ager at the time, perhaps seventeen or eighteen years of age. The gospel record shows that he was a hotheaded young man, given to sharp and impulsive speech and a tendency toward blowing off steam—hence Jesus' nickname for him and his brother James as well: "Sons of Thunder." That was our Lord's gentle way of labeling John's problem. He just kept the thunder rolling all the time.

> A Son of Thunder became an apostle of love.

Amazingly, however, "Thundering John" ultimately became the apostle of love. He became known not for his thundering but for his gentleness and goodness. We have no record that he ever married; history indicates that he devoted himself to a life of loving and serving Jesus.

John, the apostle of love, authored these three letters—1, 2, and 3 John. First John was among the last of the New Testament books to be written, and it may have been written after the gospel of John. It was penned near the close of the first century in the city of Ephesus, where John spent his later years. John wrote this epistle to Christians who were facing the dangers and trials of living in a godless world in which any selfish or sexually perverse practice was okay. It was written, in short, to people just like you and me.

The Outline of 1 John

Here is a structural overview of this letter:

The Basis of Authentic Christianity (1 John 1:1–2:27)

1.	Introduction	1:1–4
2.	Walking in the light, loving one another	1:5–2:14
3.	Avoid the love of the world, the spirit of antichrist	2:15–2:27

The Behavior of Authentic Christianity (1 John 2:28–5:21)

4.	Practicing truth, righteousness, and love	2:28–5:3
5.	Victory over the world	5:4–5
6.	Assurance of salvation	5:6–13
7.	Confidence in prayer	5:14–17
8.	Victory over habitual sin	5:18–21

Three Marks of Authentic Christianity

John's principle concern in this letter is authentic Christianity. He reminds us of the three marks of our faith that make the Christian life vital and effective: truth, righteousness, and love. These are his focus in 1 John 2:18–4:21.

But first, John describes the relationship with Jesus Christ from which flows those three personal qualities. It's a relationship of oneness with Him, a synchronization of our lives with His. Apart from that relationship, we cannot live lives characterized by truth, righteousness, and love.

The teachings of Socrates, Aristotle, Plato, Confucius, and Buddha contain the same advice for living that you find in the New Testament. In other words, if all you need is good advice, you do not need the Bible. You can get plenty of good advice from these other philosophers and religious leaders, but one thing these leaders and philosophers do not give you is the power to live out their wonderful advice. This world has enough good advice, but the power to do what we know we should do is in painfully short supply.

We all know the Golden Rule of our Lord Jesus: "Do to others as you would have them do to you." Though it is also expressed in other religions, Jesus goes a step further and empowers us to live by the Golden Rule. How does He do that? By showing us the secret of unity with Him! Fellowship with the Lord Jesus gives us the power to live out the advice He gives us. As Paul wrote in Colossians 1:27, "Christ in you, the hope of glory." The indwelling presence of Jesus, the most intimate relationship in human experience, gives us the power to live out the precepts of our faith.

First Mark: Truth

Throughout his letter, John emphasizes this fact: Jesus appeared in history. The first theme John talks about under the heading of truth is that Jesus is God and man. This message was diametrically opposed to a prevalent philosophy called Gnosticism. The nearest thing to Gnosticism today is Christian Science, which is almost pure Gnosticism. Gnostics believe that matter is evil and spirit is good and that the good human spirit is imprisoned in an evil material body. They say that the purpose of life is to teach us how to rise above the evil of our bodies and release the good spirit from it, the material body, to achieve a form of nirvana or heaven or spiritual perfection.

Jesus is God and man.

John says, in effect, "Don't be deceived by Gnostic heresy, because Jesus has come in truth. He is the God-man, eternal Spirit bonded to a human body, and anyone who denies this truth about Jesus Christ is a liar." First John was not written to refute those who were bent on destroying Christianity. No, the deception John opposed in this letter was much more subtle and crafty than any outright, fire-breathing opposition. The Gnostics simply wanted to "improve" upon Christianity. So they played down the truth of Jesus' humanity; they made subtle twists and distortions in their teaching so that their image of Jesus fit their Gnostic beliefs.

This process is still going on today. John says, "Do not be deceived. Don't be tricked by distortions in the gospel story. You will end up following a lie further and further into error, until you finally end up spiritually destroyed."

Second Mark: Righteousness

Truth is important, but it takes more to be a Christian than simply mentally assenting to a certain doctrine or creed. To our truth we must add righteousness.

Truth is meaningless if it doesn't change our behavior.

Truth is meaningless if it doesn't change our behavior. The message of John is this: If you really have Jesus Christ living in you, you can't go on living in sin, doing what is wrong, lying and stealing and living in sexual immorality. You must change your way of life. But the Gnostics said in effect, "If spirit is good and matter is evil, then the only thing that counts is the spirit. What you do with your material body doesn't matter. If you want to indulge your lusts, go ahead. It won't affect your spiritual standing with God." John responds to this error in 1 John 3:9:

No one who is born of God will continue to sin, because God's seed remains in him; he cannot go on sinning, because he has been born of God.

You cannot allow sin and the Holy Spirit to inhabit the same body. If you profess to be a Christian while living an unholy life, you are (John states bluntly) a liar.

Third Mark: Love

Truth and righteousness are difficult to master, yet these first two marks of faith are relatively easy compared with the third, love. Many Christians can say, "I know the truth and I stand on it. My doctrine is sound. And what's more, I've given up the sins and attitudes of the world. I used to drink and carouse and cheat in my business dealings and read the worst kind of magazines and see the worst kind of movies, but I don't do those things anymore." We should never minimize the changes in the life of a person who becomes truly committed to Jesus Christ, upholding His truth and forsaking sinful behavior.

But if truth and righteousness are the extent of your testimony, you'll soon find that most of the people in this world are completely unimpressed by that. Most of the things you don't do any more are things people in the world love to do and don't want to give up, so if your gospel consists of, "I have the truth, and I don't drink and smoke any more," you'll find that most people shrug and turn away. They'll say, "That's nice for you, but I like drinking and smoking, so I don't want your faith." Truth and righteousness are only two of the three aspects of an authentic Christian life.

The world is not impressed by what you *don't* do. That's negative. The world is impressed by what you *do* do. That's positive. And the positive action that impresses the world and makes our gospel attractive to the people out there is our love. That is why John says that the third mark of a genuine Christian is *love*—a special kind of love, what the New Testament Greek language calls agape love. This is love that is based on our will, not our emotions. It is a love that is based on a decision to seek the good of others, not on the fact that other people are lovable. In fact, agape love is precisely aimed at those who are hard to love!

Anyone can love someone who is lovable. It takes a special effort to love those who hate you, mistreat you, ignore you, and attack you. It takes a

> The world is not impressed by what you don't do; the world is impressed by what you do do.

special effort to love those who are wretched, suffering, smelly, dirty, poor, needy, unsightly, and unpleasant to be near. It's not hard to love those beautiful people who invite you to a lavishly catered garden party. But it takes an effort to love the toothless derelict, smelling of cheap wine, holding his paper plate in line at the downtown mission. Yet that's the kind of love God calls us to, the kind of love 1 John teaches us. It's the same kind of love that Jesus demonstrated when He reached out to the lepers, the prostitutes, the tax collectors, the poor, and when He forgave those who pounded the nails into His hands and feet, as well as the crowds who jeered Him in His dying moments. That is why John writes:

> *We love because he first loved us. If anyone says, "I love God," yet hates his brother, he is a liar. For anyone who does not love his brother, whom he has seen, cannot love God, whom he has not seen. And he has given us this command: Whoever loves God must also love his brother (4:19–21).*

Fellowship and oneness with the Lord Jesus means that we will gradually experience an opening of our hearts, like the opening of a flower in the morning sunlight. As His love shines on us, we will become more open to others, allowing the fragrance of love to drift out and attract those around us. As the power of Jesus changes us, we will grow not only in truth and righteousness but in love toward our Christian brothers and sisters and in our love toward those who are outside the faith.

Our Assurance: "We Know . . ."

The letter closes on a note of assurance: What God has told us is true and unshakable. What He has revealed about the world is absolutely certain. Three consecutive verses—1 John 5:18, 19, and 20—begin with the confident phrase, "We know." John writes:

> We know *that anyone born of God does not continue to sin; the one who was born of God keeps him safe, and the evil one cannot harm him.* We know *that we are children of God, and that the whole world is under the control of the evil one.* We know *also that the Son of God has come and has given us understanding, so that we may know him who is true. And we are in him who is true— even in his Son Jesus Christ. He is the true God and eternal life (5:18–20, emphasis added).*

We know, John says, that we are of God, that we possess the very nature and being of God, and that the whole world is in the power of the evil one. That is why the world cannot engage in agape love. The world talks about and hungers for love, but it doesn't understand the very thing it seeks, and it lacks the power to practice it because the world does not know the One who is love personified. God is love. Since we are of God, John writes, He has given us the understanding to know Him and the power to experience eternal life.

What a declaration that is! We live in an age of moral relativism, where people claim we cannot know anything for sure, where uncertainty and confusion abound. But we know. We have been given an understanding, an assurance. We are people who can stand firm and secure in a world that is falling apart.

Modern-Day Idolatry

Here is John's final word, and at first sight it may seem irrelevant in our high-tech, sophisticated age:

Dear children, keep yourselves from idols (5:21).

We don't have wooden or stone gods in our homes today, do we? We don't have to worry about idols today, do we? The fact is, we are more imperiled by idolatry today than ever before! We so easily give our devotion to things that are lower than God. Idolatry is loving anything other than God. If you took an hour to go through the register of your checkbook and your credit card statements, you could find out what some of your idols are. What do you spend your money on and what do you save your money for? What do you spend your time on? What do you think about when you wake up in the morning and when you go to bed at night? What is most important to you? Whatever it is, that is your god. If your god is not God himself, you are practicing idolatry.

For some of us, our god may be Narcissus, the god of self-love, of self-centered ambition and an obsession with success or self-beautification, of having others admire us or desire us or envy us for our beautiful possessions. For some of us, our god may be Venus, the goddess of love and sex; or Bacchus, the god of revelry and pleasure, of eating and drinking, substance abuse, and mind-altering, mood-altering drugs—as if fun and pleasure were the only reasons for living. For some of us, our god may be Mars, the god of war and competition, of vanquishing the opposition, of winning at all costs, of cutting the throats of those who oppose us, whether in business or in the church.

Prayer of Deliverance

Our prayer of deliverance from these forms of idolatry must be, "Lord, deliver me from these false gods that would rob me of my faith, of my love for humanity. Make me fall more truly in love with the Lord Jesus who alone is the only true God, who has come to give me an understanding of myself and the world around me and has come to teach me truth, righteousness, and love." The danger of idolatry is no less real for us today, in the twenty-first century, than it was for Christians in the first century, and we need to be vigilant against the taint of idolatry in our own lives.

> The danger of idolatry is no less real for us today, in the twenty-first century, than it was for Christians in the first century.

You have found the true God, John says, so keep yourselves from these secondary idols, these substitute gods that demand your attention. Give yourself completely to the One who can fulfill all your heart's desires.

NOTES

Notes

NOTES

ADVENTURING
through the
GENERAL EPISTLES

CHAPTER SEVEN

2 JOHN:
THE VITAL
BALANCE

SECOND JOHN IS THE ONLY LETTER in the New Testament that was written to a woman. We gather from the letter itself that it was written to a mother with several children, perhaps a widow, to answer her questions regarding specific problems that had arisen. In those days the people were dependent on the apostles and church leaders for truth and for answers to problems. Of course, a question then arises: How do we know if a leader who claims to speak for God actually speaks the truth? How do we distinguish between *God's* prophets and *false* prophets?

> Second John explains how we distinguish between God's prophets and false prophets.

Evidently some who claimed to be prophets had come to this woman's home, probably in the city of Ephesus, and they had raised certain doctrinal matters that disturbed her. Not knowing how to evaluate their opinions, she wrote to John and asked for his counsel. The letter we now know as 2 John is his response to her question. As we go through this letter, we will see how it also answers many questions we have today, especially the question of how to deal with people who teach spiritual concepts that are not in line with God's truth.

The Outline of 2 John

Here is an outline of this letter:

Truth and Love (2 John 1–6)

1.	John's greeting	1–3
2.	Walk in the truth of Christ	4
3.	Walk in the love of Christ	5–6

The Danger of False Teachers (2 John 7–13)

4.	How to recognize false teachers	7–9
5.	How to deal with false teachers (avoid them)	10–11
6.	Conclusion and benediction	12–13

A Balance of Truth and Love

The first six verses of the letter present both the problem and John's approach in answering it:

The elder,

To the chosen lady and her children, whom I love in the truth—and not I only, but also all who know the truth—because of the truth, which lives in us and will be with us forever:

Grace, mercy and peace from God the Father and from Jesus Christ, the Father's Son, will be with us in truth and love.

It has given me great joy to find some of your children walking in the truth, just as the Father commanded us. And now, dear lady, I am not writing you a new command but one we have had from the beginning. I ask that we love one another. And this is love: that we walk in obedience to his commands. As you have heard from the beginning, his command is that you walk in love.

Here John sets the stage for the answer to this woman's problem. He is highlighting two factors that must be taken into consideration when facing a problem of this kind: truth and love. Notice how he links these two factors in verse 3:

Grace, mercy and peace from God the Father and from Jesus Christ, the Father's Son, will be with us in truth and love *(emphasis added).*

Truth and love: These two qualities ought to characterize our lives as Christians. These are the same qualities that Paul commends to us in Ephesians 4:15—"speaking the truth in love." The great challenge we face in the Christian life is the challenge of learning to keep truth and love in balance.

> The great challenge we face in the Christian life is the challenge of learning to keep truth and love in balance.

Someone once said that a well-balanced Christian life contains salt and sugar. Salt is truth. Sugar is love. Some Christians want only the salt, and so these salty Christians go around scattering their salt wherever they go. They are all truth, no love. They are full of doctrines, dogmas, opinions, tenets, and laws. They are cold and judgmental, having no concern for the feelings, needs, or hurts of others. They defend the truth at the expense of love. In fact, they have no problem whatever speaking the truth in *cruelty!* The truth is all that matters. These people are nothing but religious saltshakers.

Saltshakers and Sugar Bowls

Others are sugar bowls. They are all love, no truth. They would never confront anyone caught in sin because that would involve telling a hard truth to that person—even if it were for that person's own good and for the good of the church. We also know of people who want to receive only sugar from their brothers and sisters; they run from the salt of truth. They say, "Give me grace, love, acceptance—but don't hold me accountable, don't confront me when I stray. If I sin, say, 'That's okay. Don't feel bad. You're okay.' Don't tell me I have to change; that's too judgmental! Don't be honest with me. Don't tell me the truth. Just be nice to me. You can keep your salt. All I want is your sugar."

Our goal as Christians should be to keep truth and love—salt and sugar—in balance. The Lord Jesus provides our perfect example. He walked in truth and love. He dealt tenderly with sinners and outcasts and truthfully with arrogant Pharisees. When He met the Samaritan woman at the well in John 4, Jesus truthfully told her all the sins she had committed, yet He dealt lovingly with her and offered living water for her thirsty soul. In John 8, after He lovingly saved the adulteress from being stoned and assured her that He did not condemn her, Jesus truthfully confronted her with her need to change. "Go," He said, "and sin no more." Jesus spoke the truth in love. He kept truth and love in perfect balance, and so should we.

Deceivers and Antichrists

In the next section, John answers the woman's question regarding the reliability of those who claim to be spiritual teachers and leaders:

> *Many deceivers, who do not acknowledge Jesus Christ as coming in the flesh, have gone out into the world. Any such person is the deceiver and the antichrist. Watch out that you do not lose what you have worked for, but that you may be rewarded fully. Anyone who runs ahead and does not continue in the teaching of Christ does not have God; whoever continues in the teaching has both the Father and the Son (vv. 7–9).*

Two Forms
of Falsehood

Two statements in this passage describe the two fundamental forms of false teaching. All Christian error and heresies arise from one of these two forms of falsehood:

Deception regarding the person of the Lord Jesus. He is the one who came from God into the world and became human; He is the only Messiah. The incarnation is an essential doctrine of Christian faith. If you trace someone's origin from birth and you discover that this person entered the stream of humanity through the normal reproductive process yet claims to be the Savior sent from God, you can disregard this person's claims. Many such false christs are in the world today, and John clearly warns us not to believe them.

Also, many people distort the truth about Jesus. One of the most common distortions is the claim that Jesus was a good person, a good moral teacher, but not truly God. This sounds nice because it's an affirmation that Jesus had many good things to say. But such a claim ignores the central message of Jesus, which was the message of himself: He claimed to be both God and human. Anyone who denies either His divinity or His humanity makes Him a liar. Anyone who denies the incarnation of the Son of God is a deceiver and does not speak for God. Such a false teacher may not be intentionally deceptive; he or she may be a deceived deceiver, but John minces no words: That person is an "antichrist," opposed to the truth about Jesus.

Deception regarding the teaching of the Lord Jesus. John says that anyone who does not continue in the doctrine or teaching of Christ does not know God (v. 9). This revealing statement addresses people who say that the Bible is not an adequate revelation of God and that we need some additional revelation from some additional teacher, guru, or book. These people may be very persuasive and sincere, but if they do not agree with the teaching of Jesus Christ, they do not know God.

Now notice the danger in these two forms of falsehood: "Watch out that you do not lose what you have worked for, but that you may be rewarded fully" (v. 8). What do you lose, as a Christian, if your faith becomes polluted by cults, heresies, and the watered-down liberal theology that is so prevalent today? Will you lose your salvation? Not if you are truly born again, of course. Salvation rests upon the work of Christ. You are not going to lose your place in heaven nor your redemption nor your part in the body of Christ. But you will lose a great deal, as John makes clear. You will lose the value of your life spent here. You will have wasted the time God gave you to serve Him effectively and obediently. Your religious activity will be revealed as nothing more than wood, hay, and stubble to be consumed in the fire of God's searching judgment. You will lose your reward.

The Danger of Falsehood

The Response to False Teachers

How, then, should we respond to those who approach us with false doctrines and heresies regarding the Lord and His teaching? John replies:

> *If anyone comes to you and does not bring this teaching, do not take him into your house or welcome him. Anyone who welcomes him shares in his wicked work (vv. 10–11).*

As we read this, remember what John has said about truth and love. Christians who are concerned about the doctrinal matters of Scripture can easily forsake the courtesy and charity that should characterize every believer. We interpret a passage like this to mean that we are to slam the door in the face of anyone who comes with a cultish tract or that we order people out of the house if they bring up some heretical teaching. If that were the case, it would be impossible even to invite neighbors, coworkers, foreign students, and the like into our homes.

John is not suggesting that our hospitality be subject to some doctrinal litmus test. We would be very offensive people if that were the case, and we would certainly have little impact in our witnessing. After all, who would we witness to if we could talk only with those who are doctrinally pure?

What, then, does John mean? He is telling us that truth should be spoken in love, and love should be bounded by truth. In other words, we are not to receive deceivers in such a way that we appear to be authenticating or accepting their teaching. In John's day, itinerant preachers and teachers stayed in private homes. The homes that received these preachers and teachers, then, served to support and subsidize their messages; thus, whoever you opened your home to was someone whose doctrine you endorsed. John is saying that we should never allow ourselves to be placed in a position where we appear to entertain, support, endorse, or subsidize the teaching of antichrist.

> **We are not to receive deceivers in such a way that we appear to be authenticating or accepting their teaching.**

John underscores the importance of his warning against receiving false teachers in verse 12, where he writes:

> *I have much to write to you, but I do not want to use paper and ink. Instead, I hope to visit you and talk with you face to face, so that our joy may be complete.*

In those days, mail was slow and uncertain, and I suppose John, like most of us, found it difficult to sit down and write letters. So he said, in effect, "I have a lot to tell you later, when I see you in person, but this matter of false teachers is so important it couldn't wait. I just had to write now to warn you about these deceivers and antichrists." Then he concludes with greetings from the Christian family he is evidently staying with, underscoring the need in Christian life for both truth and love.

Truth and love together—that is the vital balance we must seek in the Christian life. It is not only Christian balance, it is Christian sanity. A person who practices truth without love or love without truth does not have a Christian worldview. To be spiritually unbalanced is to be, in a very real sense, spiritually insane. John's goal in this brief but powerful letter is to restore us to a sane balance.

> Truth and love together—that is the vital balance we must seek in the Christian life.

NOTES

NOTES

NOTES

NOTES

CHAPTER EIGHT

3 JOHN:
BELIEVERS
and BOSSES

THIRD JOHN GIVES US an intimate glimpse into the life of the early church. It is a delightful accompaniment to the second letter, which was written to a Christian woman about how to deal with false teachers. This letter was written to a Christian man about how to care for the true teachers who traveled widely to minister God's Word and how to deal with a troubling personality type that is as common in the church today as in the first century A.D. Thus, we see both a contrast and a similarity between 2 John and 3 John.

Third John profiles three personalities in the church.

Third John gives us insight regarding the problem of personalities in the church, as illustrated by three people: Gaius (to whom this letter is written), a Christian of grace and generosity; Diotrephes, a problem personality; and Demetrius, a trustworthy and truthful Christian. These three people represent three kinds of Christians found in the church in any age.

The Outline of 3 John

Here is an outline of this letter:

Gaius Is Commended (3 John 1–8)

1.	John's greeting	1
2.	The grace (godliness) of Gaius	2–4
3.	The generosity of Gaius	5–8

Diotrephes Is Condemned (3 John 9–11)

Demetrius Is Praised (3 John 12–14)

4.	Demetrius is trustworthy and truthful	12
5.	Conclusion and benediction	13–14

Gaius: A Christian of Grace and Generosity

He was strong of soul

First, let's get to know this good man named Gaius. He may be one of three Gaiuses mentioned elsewhere in the New Testament, although Gaius was a common name in New Testament times. John evidently knew him and addresses him in a warm and friendly way. This letter portrays Gaius as a gracious and generous individual. Note three things John says about him. First, Gaius was strong of soul. John writes:

> *Dear friend, I pray that you may enjoy good health and that all may go well with you, even as your soul is getting along well (v. 2).*

That is a wonderful thing to say about someone, isn't it? "I wish you may be as strong in body as you are in your soul." It would be interesting to apply this test to people today. If your physical appearance reflected your spiritual, mental, and emotional state, what would you look like? Would you be a robust individual, strong and vital? Or would you be a doddering weakling, barely able to lift your head? Well, Gaius was the spiritually vigorous sort of person about whom John could say, "I hope your physical life is as strong as your spiritual life."

Second, Gaius was a consistent person, a man of integrity. His life matched his profession of the truth. John observes:

He lived what he professed

> *It gave me great joy to have some brothers come and tell about your faithfulness to the truth and how you continue to walk in the truth (v. 3).*

Gaius demonstrated the truth of Jesus Christ through the way he lived. He did not preach cream and live skim milk. He walked in the truth.

Third, Gaius was generous in his giving. John writes:

He was generous

> *Dear friend, you are faithful in what you are doing for the brothers, even though they are strangers to you. They have told the church about your love. You will do well to send them on their way in a manner worthy of God (vv. 5–6).*

One of the signs that a person has been genuinely touched in the heart by God is that the pocketbook loosens up. He or she becomes a cheerful giver. John says that Gaius was "faithful" in his giving. This means he was a regular and systematic giver. He gave not just when his emotions were moved, but he made a conscious habit of giving. So Gaius is commended as an open-hearted believer, full of grace and generosity.

Diotrephes: A Church Boss

Next we come to the problem personality in Gaius's church, a man named Diotrephes. John writes:

> *I wrote to the church, but Diotrephes, who loves to be first, will have nothing to do with us. So if I come, I will call attention to what he is doing, gossiping maliciously about us. Not satisfied with*

that, he refuses to welcome the brothers. He also stops those who
want to do so and puts them out of the church.
*   Dear friend, do not imitate what is evil but what is good.*
Anyone who does what is good is from God. Anyone who does what
is evil has not seen God (vv. 9–11).

This is the first example in the New Testament church of a church boss, someone who feels it is his or her job to run everything and everybody in the church. Today, a church boss could be an elder, a deacon, a pastor, or a layperson that has no official role in the church. Often, it is a wealthy, influential person, respected or even feared in the community and in the church.

Church bosses often represent the real but hidden power base of a church; while the pastor and church board may be the official leaders of the church, they may slavishly support the person or people who really call the shots. That, of course, is not how the church of Jesus Christ is supposed to function.

The early church of Gaius apparently had some kind of a membership roll. If Boss Diotrephes did not like somebody, he would scratch that person's name off the list and put him or her out of the church. This, says John, is dead wrong. Diotrephes, he explains, was guilty of four particular wrong attitudes and actions.

He was arrogant, selfish, and domineering

First and worst, Diotrephes was arrogant, selfish, and domineering. He insisted on being first in the church, an attitude that is a dead giveaway that he was acting in the flesh. This is always the demand of the flesh: "me first." In doing that, he robbed Jesus Christ of His prerogative in the church. Jesus had the right to preeminence, but it was Diotrephes who claimed the honor and glory. Unfortunately, we see plenty of people in churches today who have the spirit of Diotrephes.

One wonders if these modern versions of Diotrephes ever read 3 John and if they recognize themselves in John's description. If they do, how do they live with themselves? Dr. H. E. Robertson, an outstanding leader among the Southern Baptists and a great Greek scholar, once wrote an editorial about Diotrephes in a denominational publication. The editor of the magazine reported that twenty-five individuals from various churches wrote to cancel their subscriptions, feeling they had been personally attacked! If only such people would cancel their bossy ways instead!

He slandered John and rejected his authority

Second, the apostle says Diotrephes slandered John and rejected his authority as an apostle. "Diotrephes . . . will have nothing to do with us," says John, adding that he is continually "gossiping maliciously about us."

The apostles had a unique role in the history of the church. They were to lay the foundations of the church and were given authority to settle all questions within the church. This apostolic word—the responsibility to speak God's message to God's church—was invested in the New Testament, which is why the New Testament is so authoritative to Christians. The apostles are no longer with us, but their Spirit-inspired words have been handed down to us in God's Word. When Diotrephes slandered John and rejected his apostolic authority, he was slandering the Holy Spirit's message as spoken through John.

Third, Diotrephes refused to welcome the brethren who came in the name of the Lord speaking the truth of the Lord. Diotrephes would have nothing to do with them. He turned them aside and refused to allow them to speak in the church.

He refused to welcome those who came in the Lord's name

Fourth, Diotrephes put out of the church people who would have taken these men in. He indulged in what we would call today "secondary separation." He objected not only to the missionaries who came to the church, but he objected to those who would have received them. This has been one of the curses of the church ever since. Because of this tendency to refuse fellowship to someone who likes someone you do not like, the church is still a church divided and lacking in the power that oneness in Christ brings.

He put people out of the church who did welcome them

How, then, should we deal with church bosses? John's twofold counsel is as timely now as it was in his own day. First, church bosses should be confronted and exposed for their own good and the good of the church. "If I come," says John, "I will call attention to what he is doing, gossiping maliciously about us." The church must exercise its legitimate authority to deal with sin and pride in its ranks. If pastors or elders behave arrogantly, the other elders must confront them. If lay members behave as bosses, the church leadership must attempt to show them their error and restore them, gently and lovingly but firmly and uncompromisingly, even if it means risking the wrath of very wealthy donors. This is a matter of faith and principle, and churches must not capitulate on the basis of pragmatism, power, or dollars.

Church bosses should be confronted and exposed

The process for confronting sin in the church is found in such passages as Proverbs 27:5–6, Matthew 18:15–20, 1 Corinthians 5, and 2 Corinthians 2:1–11 (these Corinthian passages are linked and should be studied together), and Galatians 6:1–3. Although these passages don't deal specifically with the problem of church bosses, the principles are valid regardless of the nature of the sin that must be confronted.

Most important of all is John's principle of dealing with the matter openly: "I will call attention to what he is doing." Church bosses tend to operate in the shadows; when their deeds are brought into the light, they lose their power to intimidate and control.

Avoid becoming like Diotrophes

The second word of counsel John gives Gaius is to avoid becoming like Diotrephes. He does not advise Gaius to organize a split away from the church or to attempt to wrest power from Diotrephes through subtle strategies or a hidden agenda. He doesn't suggest a whisper campaign against Diotrephes. Instead, he counsels Gaius to avoid becoming contaminated by the attitude and spirit of that: "Do not imitate what is evil but what is good." If you become like Diotrephes, then he has defeated you. He has turned you away from becoming like Christ and caused you to become like him. Remember, Christ was not a boss; He was a servant.

> **Remember, Christ was not a boss; He was a servant.**

Demetrius: A Christian of Trust and Truth

The third personality we discover in 3 John is a man named Demetrius, of whom John writes:

> *Demetrius is well spoken of by everyone—and even by the truth itself. We also speak well of him, and you know that our testimony is true (v. 12).*

John writes as an apostle with the gift of discernment. He says, in effect, "I want to underscore what everybody thinks about Demetrius. Here's someone you can trust. He is a person of the truth." Demetrius was apparently the mail carrier, the bearer of this letter to Gaius, and likely was one of those missionaries who traveled from place to place. John characterized such missionaries (whom he calls "the brothers"):

> *Dear friend, you are faithful in what you are doing for the brothers, even though they are strangers to you. They have told the church about your love. You will do well to send them on their way in a manner worthy of God. It was for the sake of the Name that they went out, receiving no help from the pagans. We ought therefore to show hospitality to such men so that we may work together for the truth (vv. 5–8).*

These words describe the first group of traveling missionaries, and Demetrius was evidently one of this group. As they went from place to place, they would enjoy the hospitality of various churches. They labored as church-supported evangelists in each area, reaching out into places where the church had not yet gone.

John says three things of these missionaries: First, they have gone out; they have left behind the comforts of home. Second, they have given up income and security to obey a higher calling. Not everyone is called to missionary work. Some are called to this special task on behalf of the Lord Jesus. Others, such as Gaius, are to stay and support those who are sent out.

Missionaries like Demetrius have left the comforts of home, and they have embraced a high calling

And third, why were people like Demetrius sent out into the world? John replies, verse 7, "It was for the sake of the Name that they went out." Literally, they were sent out for the sake of the name of Jesus. The name of Jesus is very special to these Christians.

In Old Testament times, the Jews treated the name of God in a unique way. That name, Jehovah, appears throughout the Old Testament and is referred to as the Ineffable Tetragrammaton. *Ineffable* means indescribable or unutterable. *Tetragrammaton* means four letters (YHWH). Whenever the Jews encountered these four Hebrew letters for God, they did not dare speak them, so holy was the name. Even the scribe who wrote the Tetragrammaton would change pens and continue writing with a different pen. Scribes also changed their garments in reverence for God's name before they would write it. When they wrote the words of Deuteronomy 6:4—"Hear, O Israel: The LORD our God, the LORD is one"—scribes would have to change clothes twice and change pens four times to write that one line, since the Tetragrammaton occurs twice.

In the New Testament, a high measure of respect and devotion is reserved for the name of Jesus. The apostle Paul says,

God exalted him to the highest place and gave him the name that is above every name, that at the name of Jesus every knee should bow, in heaven and on earth and under the earth, and every tongue confess that Jesus Christ is Lord, to the glory of God the Father (Philippians 2:9–11).

Love for the precious name of Jesus has been the motive for sacrificial missionary efforts ever since the first century. Men and women have suffered and died for the beautiful name that people all over the world need to hear. Love for Jesus' name motivates you and me to evangelize our

They are motivated by love for the name of Jesus

neighborhoods and workplaces. Even people who are not called to go out into the world can still do a great deal to glorify and spread that name to a needy world. We can be witnesses for Jesus wherever we are, and we can be partners with the missionaries who are telling His story around the world. John says, in verse 8:

> *We ought therefore to show hospitality to such men so that we may work together for the truth.*

Now John closes his letter with a warm and personal conclusion, verses 13 and 14:

> *I have much to write you, but I do not want to do so with pen and ink. I hope to see you soon, and we will talk face to face.*
> *Peace to you. The friends here send their greetings. Greet the friends there by name.*

So ends a powerful, intimate little letter that seems as though it came not only from John, but from the Lord himself. Whenever I read these words, I feel as if I am hearing the Lord Jesus Christ say to me and to His entire church, "There is much that I'd like to say to you, but I'd rather not write it in a letter. Instead, I'm coming soon. We'll talk face-to-face then. In the meantime, I leave my peace with you. Love, your friend, Jesus."

So ends a powerful, intimate little letter that seems as though it came not only from John, but from the Lord himself.

NOTES

NOTES

NOTES

ADVENTURING
through the
GENERAL EPISTLES

CHAPTER NINE

JUDE:
CONTENDING
for the FAITH

A CLASH OF CYMBALS! A boom of tympani! A cannon blast and a cascade of fireworks! That is what the letter of Jude is like. The words of this apostle thunder from the page. Who is Jude, you ask? In the opening verse, he refers to himself simply as:

> *Jude, a servant of Jesus Christ and a brother of James.*

That clearly identifies him to the first-century reader, for Jude's brother James was well known as a leader in the early church in Jerusalem. This is the same James who wrote the epistle of James. Note that Jude, the brother of James, was also a physical half brother of the Lord Jesus. He grew up in the town of Nazareth, as did Jesus. Notice, however, that he says nothing about being physically related to the Lord. You would think that would be a credential worth putting up in neon lights, yet Jude calls himself a brother of James and a servant of Jesus Christ. Why?

I believe we can safely surmise that Jude had learned to see Jesus no longer as "my brother Jesus" but as He truly was: God poured into human flesh, the Son of God, the Savior of the world. Jude and James had a unique perspective on Jesus: They worshiped and were disciples of the one with whom they had grown up.

> **Jude expresses a unique perspective.**

As in so many other passages of the Bible, we find here yet another clear testimony of the deity of the Lord Jesus. If anyone would be in a position to refute His claim to be God, it would be Jesus' brothers. Although Jude, like James, did not come to believe in Jesus until after the resurrection, this statement at the beginning of Jude's letter is yet another seal that confirms the deity of Jesus of Nazareth.

The Outline of Jude

Here is a structural outline of Jude's epistle:

Introductory Remarks (Jude 1–4)

The Danger of False Teachers (Jude 5–16)

1.	God's past judgment of false teachers	5–7
2.	How to detect a false teacher	8–13
3.	God's future judgment of false teachers	14–16
4.	How to deal with false teachers	17–23

Benediction (Jude 24–25)

Contend for the Faith

In his introductory remarks, the apostle Jude tells us how he came to write this letter:

> *Dear friends, although I was very eager to write to you about the*
> *salvation we share, I felt I had to write and urge you to contend*
> *for the faith that was once for all entrusted to the saints (v. 3).*

He had started out to write a letter containing certain insights and understandings of the faith, and perhaps others had urged him to write his memoirs as a brother of the Lord. Then he learned about an outbreak of some false and very distasteful teaching. So Jude felt constrained by the Holy Spirit to set aside his planned treatise and to write a short, toughly worded tract instead. We don't know if the other treatise was ever written; however, this tract has become a powerfully important part of the New Testament. Here, Jude urges his readers to "contend for the faith that was once for all entrusted to the saints."

That brief statement is a powerful directive for Christians. Jude is telling us: (1) Our faith was not fabricated by people. (2) It is a single body of consistent facts. (3) It has been entrusted to the apostles whose authority is indisputable because they are inspired by God. (4) This faith was delivered once and for all; it is complete as is.

A Powerful Directive for Christians

This little letter is a dynamic, authoritative response to the claims of the cults and false doctrines of today. I believe that Jude's epistle answers every false doctrine that has ever been taught. For example, Mormonism teaches that new books, new revelations, were added since the close of the New Testament, but Jude says clearly that we are to contend for this faith that has already been delivered to us, once and for all.

> *This little letter is a dynamic, authoritative response to the claims of the cults and false doctrines of today.*

Why do we need to contend for the faith? Because false teachers have crept into the church. Jude writes:

> *Certain men whose condemnation was written about long ago*
> *have secretly slipped in among you. They are godless men, who*
> *change the grace of our God into a license for immorality and deny*
> *Jesus Christ our only Sovereign and Lord (v. 4).*

Jude is especially disturbed that these false teachers were attacking the church from within. These teachers were people who professed to be Christians. They had arisen within the church and were doing two things: (1) changing the grace of God into license to live an immoral, sexually degraded life; (2) saying that the grace of God is so broad that He will forgive anything you do. The more you sin, the more grace abounds, so go to it! This same destructive idea also pervades our society. Many people today, even within the church, claim that if you "love" someone, anything you do with that person is justified. This is not some new morality; it's an old heresy! And Jude rightly condemns it.

God's Judgment against False Teachers Is Certain

How does Jude view the problem of false teachers? First, he states that God's judgment is certain. God will not ignore those who twist His truth. Jude provides biblical evidence to support his view: God brought the people out of captivity in Egypt—over a million people, in fact. Some were believers, some were not, but God brought them all through the Red Sea and the wilderness, showing them miracle after miracle of divine protection and provision. Those who murmured and complained against God were judged; they perished in the wilderness. Those who lived by faith in God entered the Promised Land.

> God will not ignore those who twist His truth.

A second piece of evidence regarding God's judgment is the angels. The angels lived in God's presence, ministering before Him, yet some followed Satan in his rebellion. They, too, were judged. Even angels are not beyond God's judgment when they submit to pride and lust.

Jude's final piece of evidence is the cities of Sodom and Gomorrah, at the southern end of the Dead Sea, which had fallen into vile, open homosexual practices. When God's angels visited Lot, the men of the city surrounded Lot's house and ordered Lot to send his guests out to them so that they might indulge their lusts. God judged that city for its sin.

Jude reminds us that God does not take sin and rebellion lightly. He judges it. Judgment may come suddenly, as in the case of Sodom and Gomorrah, or it may be delayed, as in the case of the angels. It may even occur in the natural course of events, as in the case of those who came out of Egypt. But, whether swift or slow, God's judgment is always sure.

False teachers sin against God in three ways, as Jude says in verse 8:

In the very same way, these dreamers pollute their own bodies,
reject authority and slander celestial beings.

The Threefold Sin of False Teachers

In verses 8 to 13, Jude expands upon these three forms of sin, taking them in reverse order. He explains how the false teachers (1) slander the "celestial beings" or angels, (2) reject authority, and (3) pollute their own bodies.

First, they slander celestial beings. Jude refers to an incident unrecorded in our Bible. It comes from a book called the Assumption of Moses, which was familiar to readers of the first century. Many Christians have been troubled by this reference, because they think Jude refers to a book that has been lost from the Bible. But the book has not been lost; it still exists. It simply is not part of the accepted canon of Scripture. You can find the Assumption of Moses in most public libraries and in virtually all seminary libraries. That book, like many other non-canonical books of that time, contains a mixture of truth and error. If a New Testament writer refers back to one of these so-called lost books, a book that is not inspired Scripture, then he does so under the inspiration of the Holy Spirit, and we can be assured that the incident cited from that "lost book" is true and reliable, even if that lost book, taken as a whole, is not reliable and inspired.

Jude 14–15 includes a quotation from another lost book, the Book of Enoch, which can also be found in seminary libraries. The quotation Jude uses is valid and reliable. The entire lost book from which it was taken is not reliable; it is not Scripture.

Here is the story that Jude cites from the Assumption of Moses: When Moses died, the archangel Michael, highest of angels, disputed with the devil over the body of Moses. The devil's claim on the body of Moses was twofold: First, Moses was a murderer (he had killed an Egyptian); and, second, the body of Moses was part of the material realm, over which the devil was lord. Michael disputed the devil's demand, claiming the body for the Lord; Scripture says our bodies are important to God, and He has a plan for them as well as for our spirits.

Jude's point is this: Even so great a being as the archangel Michael would not address Satan directly but simply said, "The Lord rebuke you!" Jude's argument is that if the great archangels respect the dignity of a fallen angel, then how dare human beings speak contemptuously of the principalities and the powers in high places? Worldly people behave presumptuously when they sneer at the existence of angels or demons in Scripture.

Second, the false teachers reject authority:

Woe to them! They have taken the way of Cain; they have rushed for profit into Balaam's error; they have been destroyed in Korah's rebellion (v. 11).

Here Jude traces the way sin—especially the sin of rebellion—develops in a human life. He cites three biblical individuals as personifications of human rebellion: Cain, Balaam, and Korah. He speaks of "the way of Cain," which was essentially selfishness. Cain was the man who thought only of himself, who had no love for his brother, but put him to death. Selfishness is the first step to rebellion.

The second step is the "error of Balaam." The Old Testament contains two stories about Balaam. In one story (Numbers 22:21–35), a pagan king hired him to curse the children of Israel. As Balaam rode along on a donkey to do this, the donkey balked because it saw the angel of God blocking the way. Balaam could not see the angel, and finally the donkey had to speak with a human voice in order to rebuke the sin of this prophet.

In the second story (Numbers 31:15), Balaam again takes money, this time for sending pagan women into Israel's camp to seduce the army and introduce idol worship and sexual rites. Balaam would do anything to gain money, even curse Israel and lead Israel into sin and judgment. His sin is greed and leading others astray, and that is the error of Balaam. When a person teaches someone else to sin, the result is multiplied judgment on the teacher.

> When a person teaches someone else to sin, the result is multiplied judgment on the teacher.

Jesus said to his disciples: "Things that cause people to sin are bound to come, but woe to that person through whom they come. It would be better for him to be thrown into the sea with a millstone tied around his neck than for him to cause one of these little ones to sin" (Luke 17:1–2).

From the selfishness of Cain to the sin of Balaam—greed and leading others into sin—false teachers descend to the sin of Korah: defiant rebellion. Korah and his followers opposed Moses and Aaron in the wilderness. In Numbers 16:1–3 we read:

*Korah . . . and certain Reubenites . . . became insolent and rose
up against Moses. With them were 250 Israelite men, well-known
community leaders who had been appointed members of the council.
They came as a group to oppose Moses and Aaron and said to them,
"You have gone too far! The whole community is holy, every one of
them, and the LORD is with them. Why then do you set yourselves
above the LORD's assembly?"*

Korah blatantly challenged the God-given authority of Moses and
Aaron. In response, God told Moses and the rest of the people to sepa-
rate themselves from Korah and his band. When Moses and the people
had moved a safe distance away, the ground opened beneath Korah and
the other rebels, and they went down alive into the pit. This was God's
dramatic way of warning against the grievous, damnable sin of defiance of
God-given authority.

Third, the false teachers defile the flesh.

As you read along in this letter, you hear Jude getting more and more
worked up, like a backwoods preacher on revival night. At this point, the
apostle really begins to thunder. He growls that these false teachers are
blemishes on the Christians' agape-love feasts that lead the people into
riotous carousing. The agape-love feasts were actually potluck suppers
where the early Christians would gather and bring food with them to the
Sunday worship service. After the service, they would all partake together;
they called this a love feast. What a blessed name! I love potluck suppers,
but I would much rather we returned to the original Christian name for
them: love feasts.

These feasts were wonderful times of fellowship, but they began to dete-
riorate as people divided into cliques. Some kept the bucket of chicken
for themselves, others kept the angel food cake, and
soon there was division. Instead of love, these feasts
began to celebrate selfishness. The false teachers were
the most selfish of all—taking and partaking, giving
nothing, looking only after themselves.

As Jude goes on, he adds imagery upon imagery,
much as James does in his epistle and as Jesus does
in His parables. In verses 12 and 13, Jude describes
these useless teachers as waterless clouds (promising
rain, delivering nothing); fruitless trees (promising fruit, producing
nothing); twice dead (dead not only in Adam, but dead in Christ as well,

> The false teachers were
> the most selfish of all—
> taking and partaking,
> giving nothing, looking
> only after themselves.

since they have rejected Him); wild waves of the sea, casting up the foam of their own shame; and wandering stars in the eternal darkness.

In verses 14 and 15, Jude quotes Enoch, from the lost Book of Enoch that I mentioned earlier, predicting the judgment that is coming upon the false teachers. In verse 16, Jude describes them as grumblers, malcontents, following their own passions, loud-mouthed boasters flattering people to gain advantage. These words sting us because we see aspects of ourselves in this description, don't we?

Finally, after thundering, shouting, and pounding the pulpit, Jude comes to a pause. As the echoes of his last shout fade in the air, he drops his voice, leans close to us, and says softly,

> *Dear friends, remember what the apostles of our Lord Jesus Christ foretold. They said to you, "In the last times there will be scoffers who will follow their own ungodly desires." These are the men who divide you, who follow mere natural instincts and do not have the Spirit.*
>
> *But you, dear friends, build yourselves up in your most holy faith and pray in the Holy Spirit. Keep yourselves in God's love as you wait for the mercy of our Lord Jesus Christ to bring you to eternal life (vv. 17–21).*

In other words, "The apostles predicted these deceivers would rise up among you and try to divide you. This comes as no surprise. So, my friends, what are you going to do about it?"

Four Responses to False Teachers

Jude goes on to commend four responses to us. The first way we respond to false teachers is this: Build yourselves up in the most holy faith; *know the truth*. We have to learn what the truth is, and that means we must study the Bible. Notice, Jude doesn't call for a counterinsurgency against the false teachers. He doesn't call for an inquisition or a lynching of these deceivers. His solution is not a negative; it's a positive. He says, "Fight lies with the truth! Know the truth, and the lies will never harm you."

> We have to learn what the truth is, and that means we must study the Bible.

The second way we must respond to false teachers is to *pray in the Spirit*. To pray in the Holy Spirit means to pray according to His teaching and in His power, depending upon God. Study and learn what prayer is; follow the teaching of Scripture about it. Obey the Holy Spirit in your prayer life.

The third way we respond to false teachers is by *keeping ourselves in the love of God.* Jude is saying to us, "God's love is just like the sunshine, constantly shining on you. But you can put up barriers to shade yourself from His love. Don't do that! Keep yourself in the bright sunshine of His love. Keep walking in the experience of His goodness." We must constantly purge sin from our lives through confession, allowing His love and forgiveness to continually flow through our hearts, filling our lives. When we choose to hide in the shadows, His love is out there, but we remain dark and cold by our own choosing. He loves us whether we are in fellowship with Him or not, but when we walk in communion with Him, we experience and feel the warmth of His love.

> We must constantly purge sin from our lives through confession, allowing His love and forgiveness to continually flow through our hearts, filling our lives.

The fourth and final way to respond to false teachers is to *wait for the mercy of our Lord Jesus Christ to eternal life.* This refers to our expectation of the second coming of Christ. We must keep our hope bright and alert, looking for Jesus to intervene in history, bringing to an end the age of sin and suffering. Our prayer of expectation is, "Your kingdom come, your will be done in earth as it is in heaven." Come, Lord Jesus.

Jude concludes his letter with some practical instruction in how to meet the spiritual needs of those around us:

> *Be merciful to those who doubt; snatch others from the fire and save them; to others show mercy, mixed with fear—hating even the clothing stained by corrupted flesh (vv. 22–23).*

Conclusion: Show Mercy to Those around You

What does Jude mean, "Be merciful to those who doubt"? He wants us to be understanding, not judgmental, toward those who struggle in their faith. A person who has questions or doubts about the Christian faith should not be treated as an unbeliever or an enemy of the faith or as a person who is sinning. So don't condemn such people. Instead, answer their questions, reason with them, love them.

He then addresses the problem of Christians who have become a danger to themselves because of sinful attitudes and behavior. These we must snatch from the fire, if possible. We must love them enough to try to pull them back from the brink of disaster, if possible. But note that Jude says our mercy should be "mixed with fear—hating even the clothing stained by corrupted flesh."

We must always remember that it is easier for a falling person to pull us down than for us to pull that person up. Risk is involved when we reach out to someone who is tumbling into the fire, and it is not always possible to save someone who is determined to continue the slide into sin and judgment. We cannot save a person who chooses not to be saved. If you feel that person pulling you into the fire, you must let go and save yourself. You are not responsible for another person's bad choices. Save the falling brother or sister if possible, but if it is not possible, at least save yourself.

Jude closes with these words:

> *To him who is able to keep you from falling and to present you before his glorious presence without fault and with great joy—to the only God our Savior be glory, majesty, power and authority, through Jesus Christ our Lord, before all ages, now and forevermore! Amen (vv. 24–25).*

A Glowing— and Sobering— Benediction

This is one of the most glowing benedictions in the New Testament. It is also a sobering benediction. Jude states that God is able to keep us from falling, but this very statement suggests the possibility that we could fall if we choose to. He is able to keep us from falling, but He does not guarantee that we will not fall. The choice of whether to fall or stand is ours. If we will only obey God, He will keep us from falling.

Jude also states that God is able to present us without fault and with great joy. God has so completely dealt with sin that He is able to wipe our sins completely away and to present us faultless before His glory.

All majesty and dominion belong to God from before creation to beyond the end of the world.

Finally, Jude exalts the only God, our Savior, the Lord Jesus Christ, and offers to Him glory, majesty, power, and authority from before all time and now and forever. All majesty and dominion belong to God from before creation to beyond the end of the world. The entire universe, all of time and space, gathers about Him and worships Him. That is the God we serve and trust. That is the faith for which we contend.

NOTES

NOTES

NOTES

CHAPTER TEN

REVELATION: THE END— *and a* NEW BEGINNING

WHAT IS IT THAT MAKES US want to read the last chapter of a book first? For some reason, many people begin reading the Bible with the book of Revelation, and that's usually a mistake. While it is vivid, dramatic, and exciting, this book plunges you into a confusing swirl of dragons and trumpets, vials and seals, symbols and Old Testament imagery. Someone who begins with Revelation might well give up the whole Bible in frustration over trying to make any sense of Revelation. Without a background in both the Old and New Testaments, this book will certainly leave you baffled.

> This book shows us how all the events of the past several thousand years are actually moving toward a single event: the return of Jesus Christ to establish His kingdom.

But the book of Revelation is not impossible to understand. Someone who is familiar with the rest of the Bible will be able to relate events in Revelation to the entire prophetic pattern of God's Word; with careful, patient study, it will make sense. Revelation is the capstone of the Bible, strategically placed at the end of the Bible. It is the climax of the entire revelation of God to His people. It is also the lens through which human history and Bible prophecy begin to come into focus and make sense. This book shows us how all the events of the past several thousand years are actually moving toward a single event: the return of Jesus Christ to establish His kingdom.

The book of Revelation is the only prophecy book in the New Testament. However, other New Testament books do contain prophetic passages. The Gospels contain prophetic utterances of Jesus, and the prophetic revelations given to Paul are found primarily in his letters to the Thessalonians. Nonetheless, Revelation is the only book in the New Testament that is primarily devoted to prophecy.

The title of the book is contained in the first verse of the book:

"The revelation of Jesus Christ . . .

Notice, it is not Revelations, plural. This is a singular revelation of a singular person, Jesus Christ. John continues:

. . . which God gave him to show his servants what must soon take place. He made it known by sending his angel to his servant John (1:1).

God the Father gave this revelation to Jesus Christ. Jesus then revealed it to John through an angel. The purpose of this revelation is to show the Lord's servants—that's you and me and all other followers of Christ—what must soon take place. This book was written by the apostle John when he was a captive on the island of Patmos in the Aegean Sea. It dates from about A.D. 95. John says that he was in the Spirit on the Lord's Day, and he began to see visions of things that must soon come to pass. So this is clearly a predictive book.

God's Use of Symbols in Revelation

Notice that statement at the end of 1:1: "He made it known by sending his angel." The words, "He made it known" are a translation of a Greek word that means "He signified it." Notice that the word *signified* can be broken down this way: "He sign-ified it." That is, God made this revelation known by signs, by symbols.

Why did God use symbols? Why didn't He reveal the future in plain language? One reason is that He was dealing with future events, which were beyond the imagination and understanding of men and women of the first century: nuclear warfare, worldwide plagues, biological warfare, information technologies, and space technologies. How could these concepts be explained to a generation who knew nothing about computers, missiles, nuclear energy, Stealth fighters, or helicopters?

Explaining Modern Technologies to First-Century People

Another helpful thing to understand about these symbols is that they are consistent with symbols found in other prophetic passages of the Bible. They are part of the overall prophetic tapestry of Scripture. So if you want to understand Revelation, you should begin by comparing Revelation with Daniel, Ezekiel, and other parts of the Old and New Testaments.

Revelation's Symbols: Part of the Prophetic Tapestry of Scripture

I believe the Holy Spirit knew that this book would be difficult for many, so we find these words at the beginning of the book:

> *Blessed is the one who reads the words of this prophecy, and blessed are those who hear it and take to heart what is written in it, because the time is near (1:3).*

We who seek God's blessing on our lives and who want to understand the shape of things to come are eager to understand the symbols and the substance of God's book of Revelation.

Do 4 | 1:2
7 spirits

The Background of the Book of Revelation

The book of Revelation is addressed, first of all, to the seven churches in Asia Minor (present-day Turkey). The first section of the book consists of seven letters to these seven churches. There were more than seven churches in that region, of course, but these seven churches were selected because they were representative of the churches of every era, including ours. These letters come not from the apostle John, but from the triune God who has inspired these words. In Revelation 1:4–5, John sets forth the triune nature of the divine author of these letters, although they must be read carefully to be understood:

> These seven churches were selected because they were representative of the churches of every era, including ours.

> *John,*
> *To the seven churches in the province of Asia:*
> *Grace and peace to you from him who is, and who was, and who is to come [that's God the Father], and from the seven spirits before his throne [signifying the Holy Spirit in His sevenfold plenitude of power], and from Jesus Christ [the Son], who is the faithful witness, the firstborn from the dead, and the ruler of the kings of the earth.*

Father, Son, and Holy Spirit jointly gave to seven churches—and to us—these seven letters, as well as the amazing prediction that follows. As is the case with most modern books, the ancient book of Revelation contains a dedication:

> *To him who loves us and has freed us from our sins by his blood, and has made us to be a kingdom and priests to serve his God and Father—to him be glory and power for ever and ever! Amen (1:5–6).*

The book is dedicated to Jesus Christ, the one who laid the foundation for all human blessing. Next, the theme of the book is introduced:

> *Look, he is coming with the clouds, and every eye will see him, even those who pierced him; and all the peoples of the earth will mourn because of him. So shall it be! Amen (1:7).*

Acts
3:1-9

Corinth Theas
5:7 13-17 ①

This is a book about the second coming of Jesus Christ—how it will be accomplished, the events on earth that accompany this event, and what will happen afterward. The Lord then adds His personal signature as the book's author:

"I am the Alpha and the Omega," says the Lord God, "who is, and who was, and who is to come, the Almighty" (1:8).

This book was written during a time of intense persecution of the church, during the reign of the vicious Roman emperor Domitian, who declared himself lord and god of the Roman people. The Christians of the time were desperate for encouragement and assurance, so they welcomed this message from the Lord, the one who is the Alpha and the Omega, the beginning and the end. They needed to hear that all of history, including their time of suffering, was under His control.

> John's audience needed to hear that all of history, including their time of suffering, was under God's control.

The Outline and Divisions of the Book of Revelation

The framework for the book is given in verse 19, where John records what the Lord told him: "Write, therefore, what you have seen, what is now and what will take place later." Then the book falls into three divisions: (1) the things John saw—chapter 1; (2) current conditions as expressed in the seven letters to seven churches—chapters 2 and 3; and (3) things that will take place later—chapters 4 through 22.

I believe that the phrase "what will take place later" refers to the events following the departure of the church. While chapters 2 and 3 cover the entire present age (from John's time to our own), all of the chapters that follow concern the culmination of human events. Elsewhere in the Bible this startling event is called the Great Tribulation, or the time of the end, or Daniel's Seventieth Week. All the frightening turbulence of our own day is moving toward this event, and in this chapter we will touch briefly on some of the highlights of this unfolding of God's plan.

Here is a brief structural overview of this amazing book:

What You Have Seen (Revelation 1)

1. Introduction   1:1–8
2. The Revelation of Christ   1:9–20

What Is Now (Revelation 2–3)

3. The Lord's letter to Ephesus   2:1–7
4. The Lord's letter to Smyrna   2:8–11
5. The Lord's letter to Pergamum   2:12–17
6. The Lord's letter to Thyatira   2:18–29
7. The Lord's letter to Sardis   3:1–6
8. The Lord's letter to Philadelphia   3:7–13
9. The Lord's letter to Laodicea   3:14–22

What Will Take Place Later (Revelation 4–22)

10. The throne of God and the Lamb/Lion   4
11. The sealed book   5
12. Prophecies of the great tribulation   6:1–19:6
     A. The seven seals of judgment   6:1–8:5
     – B. The seven trumpets of judgment   8:6–11:19
     C. Prophecies of the woman, the beast,   12:1–14:20
         the 144,000, and the harvest judgment
     ⌐ D. The seven vials (bowls) of judgment   15:1–16:21
     E. The great harlot overthrown   17
     F. The destruction of mystery Babylon   18:1–19:3
13. Prophecies of the second coming of Christ   19:4–21
14. Prophecies of the millennium; the reign of   20
     the saints while Satan is bound for a
     thousand years, ending in the great white
     throne judgment
15. Prophecies of the new heaven, the new earth, 21:1–22:5
     and the New Jerusalem
16. Conclusion, benediction, and prayer: 22:6–21
     "Come, Lord Jesus"

Seven Letters to Seven Churches

In chapters 2 and 3, we have the letters to the seven churches. These letters should be viewed on three levels. First, they are addressed to actual churches and deal with actual problems in those churches. Second, these churches symbolize individual churches during any time in history; your own church undoubtedly fits the pattern of one of these churches. Third, these churches represent the seven stages in the process of the history of the church, from the first century until today. Let's look at each of these letters and churches.

The church in Ephesus (2:2–7) was outwardly successful but was beginning to lose its first love, that driving motivation so necessary for effectiveness in the Christian life. When we look at this letter from the viewpoint of church history, we see that many churches began to lose their first love during the period immediately following the death of the apostles. The Ephesian period of church history covers the years from A.D. 70, when the temple at Jerusalem was destroyed, to about A.D. 160. During that time, literally hundreds of churches had drifted from their warm, compassionate ministry to the world toward a formal, unloving institutional religion. The church became rife with conflict and theological arguments.

Letter 1, Ephesus: Losing Its First Love

The word *Smyrna* means "myrrh," a fragrant spice or perfume obtained when the tender bark of the flowering myrrh tree is pierced or crushed. It is a fitting name for the first-century church of Smyrna (2:8–11), which gave off a fragrance of Christ throughout the region because it was a church that was often afflicted. Historically, the church in Smyrna represents a period called the Age of Martyrs, which lasted from about A.D. 160 to the rise of the first so-called Christian emperor, Constantine the Great, in A.D. 324. To call this period the Age of Martyrs is not to suggest that this was the only time in history when Christians have been martyred, but these particular Christians were persecuted with unequaled cruelty.

Letter 2, Smyrna: Giving off a Fragrance of Christ in Its Frequent Afflictions

Pergamum means "married." This church (2:12–17) had married the world; it was trying to cohabitate with the godless world system. All the attitudes and value systems of an unbelieving world had infiltrated the processes of the church. The Pergamum stage of church history is that period of time between the accession of Constantine the Great in A.D. 324 to the sixth century, when the era of the popes began. This was the time of the first "marriage" between church and state, when Constantine made Christianity the official religion of the Roman Empire. During this time in its history, the church was enjoying considerable popularity. It had come to be viewed not so much as a family of faith but as a formal worldly kingdom, much like any other kingdom. As the church's political influence grew, its spiritual influence waned.

Letter 3, Pergamum: Accommodating Itself to a Godless World System

The church in Thyatira (2:18–29) was going through a period of spiritual adultery. It had lost its purity and needed to purify itself lest the Lord himself purify it through a painful process of discipline. It was the most corrupt of the seven churches and symbolized a dark and corrupt period in Christian history: the Dark Ages, a period when the church lost its zeal and purity, when it became infiltrated with superstition and paganism.

Letter 4, Thyatira: The Most Corrupt of the Seven Churches

The Dark Ages lasted from the seventh century to the sixteenth century, when the Reformation began.

Letter 5, Sardis: Christians in Name Only

The church in Sardis (3:1–6) had rediscovered the truth, but it lacked vitality. The church had built up a good reputation, but it was really dead and corrupt inside. Today, we would call the Christians at Sardis "nominal Christians"—*nominal* from the root word for "name." The Christians at Sardis were Christians in name only. Jesus told them, "You have a reputation, a name for being alive, but you are dead!" Apparently, the church at Sardis was largely made up of people who outwardly professed Christ but who possessed no real spiritual life. This is a picture of the period of the Reformation, from the sixteenth century to the eighteenth century. Although the Reformation churches began in a flaming fire of zeal, they soon died down to the whitened ashes of a dead orthodoxy.

Letter 6, Philadelphia: True and Faithful to the Word

The church of Philadelphia (3:7–13) is a wonderful church. The Lord has no criticism whatsoever of this church. He commends the Philadelphia church because it is true and faithful to the Word. It has a little strength, He says, speaking of the quiet inner strength of the Holy Spirit, as contrasted with the overt power of the world's political structure. This church typifies the church age of the nineteenth century, the great evangelical awakening, when the Christian church focused less on acquiring political power and more on obeying its inner strength, the Holy Spirit. The church of this era was stirred to action, and it expanded into the far corners of the earth in a great missionary movement.

Letter 7, Laodicea: Materially Rich but Spiritually Poor

The church of Laodicea (3:14–22), the rich church, says, "We don't need anything at all from God. We've got money, influence, power. That's all we need." And God says, "You blind fools! Don't you know you don't have anything—that you are wretched and poor, pitiable and blind? Buy from me gold refined by fire." The Lord pictures himself standing outside the door of the church, knocking for admittance. "You are neither cold nor hot," says the Lord. The Laodiceans were not like the church at Sardis, which was as cold as death. Nor were they like the church at Philadelphia, which was hot, alive, and vital. They were merely lukewarm.

> As both history and prophecy clearly confirm, Laodicea symbolizes the church of the last age—our own age.

Each of the seven churches of Revelation represents a specific time in church history. Looking back across twenty centuries of church history, we can see how accurate each of these prophetic symbols has been. As both history and prophecy clearly confirm, Laodicea symbolizes the church of the last age—our own age. Yes, the fact is that we live in Laodicean times, when the church considers itself rich but is poor; when it is lukewarm, neither hot nor cold.

Of course, this is a generalization. We see many vital, alive Christians, even in our lukewarm age. Our challenge and our task are to make sure that we live as Philadelphian Christians even in this Laodicean age. Even if every other church around us seems infected with Laodiceanism, we can still choose to burn brightly and hotly, giving off the light of Jesus in this twilight age of the church. If we do so, then Jesus says that the concluding promise of Revelation 3 is ours:

> *"To him who overcomes, I will give the right to sit with me on my throne, just as I overcame and sat down with my Father on his throne. He who has an ear, let him hear what the Spirit says to the churches" (3:21–22).*

What Will Take Place Later

The book takes a sudden turn at chapter 4. Notice the key phrase in verse 2: "in the Spirit." This phrase occurs four times in Revelation: in 1:10, where John is on the isle of Patmos and hears the trumpet-like voice that introduces this entire vision; here, in 4:2; in 17:3, when an angel carries him into the desert where he sees the woman sitting on the scarlet beast; and also in 21:10, when John is carried to a mountain and shown the Holy City, the New Jerusalem, coming down out of heaven. Each time John is "in the Spirit," it signals that something highly significant is happening.

> *At once I was in the Spirit, and there before me was a throne in heaven with someone sitting on it (4:2).*

This juncture is significant because the scene shifts now from earth to heaven. By heaven, I don't mean somewhere out in space. In the Bible, heaven is the realm of the invisible—another dimension, if you like, wherein God reigns hidden from our eyes but present among us. It is a spiritual kingdom that surrounds us on every side but one we cannot taste or touch or see; yet it is utterly real, more real than this plane of existence that we call real life. What we think of as reality is a mere vapor compared with the reality of the heavenly realm.

This kingdom of heaven was opened to John, and he saw a throne and the one who sat upon it. Immediately he knew who it was; he did not need to be told. It was the throne of God, and God was in control of all history. John saw a remarkable vision of the powerlessness and the weakness of humanity contrasted with the vast might and authority of God.

The Lamb Turned Lion

John then saw a Lamb standing in front of the throne—a Lamb with its throat cut. That may seem a strange symbol for the Son of God, but it is a very apt one—a slaughtered innocent lamb, a sacrifice. As John watched, the Lamb turned into a Lion, and John saw that this Lamb-turned-Lion was also the king of all. He stood before the one upon the throne, who held in His hand a little book. This little book is enormously significant in the book of Revelation: It is God's program for the establishment of His kingdom on earth. In heaven, God rules unchallenged; on earth, His will is constantly being challenged by puny people who dare to lift their fists against the Creator-God of the universe. But God is going to change all that, and He is going to do so by means of the Lamb who is the Lion, the one who alone has the right to take the book (actually, a scroll) and open it.

The Opening of the Scroll

And as the seven seals of this book are loosened, the scroll unrolls until at last its text is plain to all. John weeps as he first sees the scroll because he thinks that no one has the right to open it. But then he sees the Son of Man, and he knows that Jesus alone is entitled to unfold the scroll that will produce God's kingdom on earth.

The Seven Seals

As the scroll unfolds, we see that there are seven seals. Notice that the number seven appears frequently in this book; it is always a significant number. We have already seen the seven churches. Now we see seven seals, each one revealing a new power at work on earth. These are followed by seven trumpets and then seven vials (or bowls) full of God's wrath.

The Beginning of the Tribulation

In Revelation 6, we witness the beginning of this seven-year period that, the prophet Daniel tells us, is the culmination of history. All the worldwide events of our present day are moving toward this seven-year period called the Great Tribulation. This cataclysmic event will be ushered in by a worldwide preaching of the gospel, as we learn from our Lord's talk to the disciples on the Mount of Olives:

> *"This gospel of the kingdom will be preached in the whole world as a testimony to all nations, and then the end will come"* (Matthew 24:14).

The book of Revelation first considers the church as a unit, then turns to historical events concerning the rest of the world. In light of this, I believe that the church is caught up to be with the Lord prior to the period of the seven-year tribulation.

The first event of that age is the worldwide preaching of the gospel, symbolized by the first of these seven seals:

> *I looked, and there before me was a white horse! Its rider held a bow, and he was given a crown, and he rode out as a conqueror bent on conquest (6:2).*

White always symbolizes divinity and deity; it represents purity and holiness. The bow represents conquest. This is a picture of the gospel's conquest of the world.

The First Seal

The second seal means war. John writes:

The Second Seal

> *Another horse came out, a fiery red one. Its rider was given power to take peace from the earth and to make men slay each other. To him was given a large sword (6:4).*

Could that great sword symbolize the terrible power of nuclear weapons? Or even conventional warfare on a previously unimagined scale?

The third seal and the third horseman symbolize famine, which is inevitable in the wake of worldwide war.

The Third Seal

The fourth seal and the fourth horseman bring calamitous death by four means—sword, famine, plague, and wild beasts:

The Fourth Seal

> *I looked, and there before me was a pale horse! Its rider was named Death, and Hades was following close behind him. They were given power over a fourth of the earth to kill by sword, famine and plague, and by the wild beasts of the earth (6:8).*

In the second, third, and fourth seals, John describes the forces at work in humanity to produce the events of history in the last days. Human power is therefore prominent throughout this time, and we see that God allows the sinful human race to unleash horrible events.

The fifth seal is an expression of the inward power of humanity, the prayer of the martyrs. This is followed by cosmic disturbances, which provide a key to the entire book:

The Fifth Seal

I watched as he opened the sixth seal. There was a great earthquake. The sun turned black like sackcloth made of goat hair, the whole moon turned blood red, and the stars in the sky fell to earth, as late figs drop from a fig tree when shaken by a strong wind. The sky receded like a scroll, rolling up, and every mountain and island was removed from its place (6:12–14).

The Sixth Seal The earthquake in this passage gives us a clue to understanding this book. The final event previewed here in the sixth seal is marked by a great earthquake, hail, and fire. This event signals the end of the seven-year period Jesus described when He said, "Immediately after the distress of those days 'the sun will be darkened, and the moon will not give its light; the stars will fall from the sky, and the heavenly bodies will be shaken' " (Matthew 24:29). This will happen just before Jesus Christ returns with His church.

The Seventh Seal The seventh seal summarizes the events of the last half of this seven-year period, unfolded in Revelation 10 and 11, where we again encounter the earthquake when the seventh trumpet sounds:

Then God's temple in heaven was opened, and within his temple was seen the ark of his covenant. And there came flashes of lightning, rumblings, peals of thunder, an earthquake and a great hailstorm (11:19).

The Woman, the Beast, and the Dragon

Chapters 12 through 14 introduce to us larger-than-life characters who act out the drama on earth. First, a woman (easily recognizable as Israel) brings forth a man-child, whom history has already informed us is the Son of God. Against Him in a great conflict are arrayed the angels of the devil and the great dragon called Satan. As John watches, a beast rises up out of the sea, and John recognizes that the beast is a form of human government linked to Rome, the fourth great world kingdom spoken of by Daniel. In some form, the Roman Empire is to exist until the end of time.

If you look at our Western world, you can see how true that is. Every nation of the Western hemisphere was settled by a member nation of the Roman Empire. We are Roman to the core; the whole Western world is Roman in its thought, philosophy, and attitude. Associated with this beast out of the sea is another beast, or religious leader, who rises out of the earth and whom many link with the antichrist.

The Vials of God's Wrath

Chapters 14 through 16 largely deal with the description of the vials of God's wrath, which are exactly the same as those terrible judgments of which Jesus spoke when He said the sun would be darkened, the moon turned to blood, and God's wrath would be poured out upon the earth.

In the latter part of chapter 16 and continuing through chapters 17 and 18, you find the judgment of the great religious harlot called "MYSTERY BABYLON THE GREAT." Babylon was the source of ancient idolatry and is used as a symbol of what we might call "religious godlessness"— something that looks godly and spiritual but is essentially godless. It is a religion that exercises political power through religious authority.

The Judgment of Babylon the Great

If you read this passage carefully, you will see that this mystery Babylon is not any one system, institution, or denomination but rather an attitude that permeates the entire church. Wherever you find anyone acting religiously, trying to gain political power or authority, you have mystery Babylon, and it is found in all

This mystery Babylon is not any one system, institution, or denomination but rather an attitude that permeates the entire church.

churches. As Jesus said, referring to the weeds planted among the good wheat, "Let both grow together until the harvest" (Matthew 13:30). And in Revelation 19, you have the harvest (as predicted in chapter 14):

> *I looked, and there before me was a white cloud, and seated on the cloud was one "like a son of man" with a crown of gold on his head and a sharp sickle in his hand. Then another angel came out of the temple and called in a loud voice to him who was sitting on the cloud, "Take your sickle and reap, because the time to reap has come, for the harvest of the earth is ripe" (14:14–15).*

This harvest occurs when Jesus Christ returns to earth:

The Harvest

> *I saw heaven standing open and there before me was a white horse, whose rider is called Faithful and True. With justice he judges and makes war. His eyes are like blazing fire, and on his head are many crowns. He has a name written on him that no one knows but he himself. He is dressed in a robe dipped in blood, and his name is the Word of God. The armies of heaven were following him, riding on white horses and dressed in fine linen, white and*

clean. Out of his mouth comes a sharp sword with which to strike down the nations. "He will rule them with an iron scepter." He treads the winepress of the fury of the wrath of God Almighty (19:11–15).

Armageddon   By this time, all the nations of the earth have gathered in that battlefield called Armageddon, in the land of Israel, and this is where the Son of God appears with the armies of heaven. Now at last, all the supernatural forces—forces that human beings have so long and arrogantly denied—suddenly reveal themselves to human eyes in such a way as to eliminate all the opposition of entrenched evil against the will and authority of God.

A New Heaven and a New Earth

The book closes as the Son of God sets up His kingdom on earth, as He had promised. After the judgment of the dead comes a new heaven and a new earth, and the city of God, the New Jerusalem, descends from heaven. There, God makes His habitation with the human race. It is the fulfillment of the prayer Jesus taught us to pray: "Your kingdom come, your will be done on earth as it is in heaven" (Matthew 6:10).

This city is astoundingly beautiful. John sees no temple in it, for it does not need a temple, nor does it need the sun or moon to shine upon it. The light within it is the presence of God himself. Its gates shall never be shut by day or by night. The entire universe is at last cleansed of human rebellion, and there is nothing to be feared. All the beautiful dreams of the prophets are fulfilled at this time. Swords are transformed into plowshares and spears into hooks for pruning the fruit-laden trees. War no longer exists.

> The entire universe is at last cleansed of human rebellion, and there is nothing to be feared.

At the end of the book, we are admonished to wait for the coming of Jesus and to work for it, to be diligent and faithful and obedient until the Son of God comes. You may be surprised to know that this is a book of extreme optimism. Although Revelation is better known for its scenes of death, horror, upheaval, and mass destruction, it truly does not stop there. Revelation looks beyond the Tribulation, beyond Armageddon, all the way to the final victory of God, more sure than tomorrow's sunrise. C. S. Lewis writes this commentary on that glorious coming day:

God is going to invade, all right: but what is the good of saying you are on His side then, when you see the whole natural universe melting away like a dream and something else—something it never entered your head to conceive—comes crashing in; something so beautiful to some of us and so terrible to others that none of us will have any choice left? For this time it will be God without disguise; something so overwhelming that it will strike either irresistible love or irresistible horror into every creature. It will be too late then to choose your side. There is no use saying you choose to lie down when it has become impossible to stand up. That will not be the time for choosing: it will be the time when we discover which side we really have chosen, whether we realized it before or not. Now, today, this moment, is our chance to choose the right side. God is holding back to give us that chance. It will not last for ever. We must take it or leave it (*Mere Christianity*, [1943; reprint, New York: Macmillan, 1960], 66).

Revelation is filled with encouragement. It is a book that will either inspire your faith or fill you with fear. It will give you great comfort and encouragement if you know the Lord of all time and all space. But it is also a solemn book designed to make us understand that the one who unrolls the scroll is the one who was once here, the one who died on Calvary's cross, the Lamb led to slaughter so that He might win the right to be the Lion, the king of all the earth.

The Lord is coming, and it won't be long now. Those who know Him welcome that day and work and pray to hasten it. People who don't know Him either scoff at that day or dread it. The book of Revelation concludes with this promise of Jesus himself:

> *He who testifies to these things says, "Yes, I am coming soon."*
> *Amen. Come, Lord Jesus.*
> *The grace of the Lord Jesus be with God's people. Amen (22:20).*

NOTES

NOTES

NOTES

NOTES

NOTE TO THE READER

The publisher invites you to share your response to the message of this book by writing Discovery House Publishers, P.O. Box 3566, Grand Rapids, MI 49501, U.S.A. For information about other Discovery House books, music, videos, or DVDs, contact us at the same address or call 1-800-653-8333. Find us on the Internet at **http://www.dhp.org/** *or send e-mail to* **books@dhp.org.**